The Special Messenger

The Special Messenger
Rediscovering Kierkegaard

Alastair Hannay
University of Oslo

humming earth

Published by
humming earth
an imprint of
Zeticula Ltd
Unit 13
196 Rose Street
Edinburgh
EH2 4AT
Scotland

http://www.hummingearth.com
admin@hummingearth.com

Text Copyright © Robert Alastair Hannay 2022
First published January 2022

ISBN 978-1-84622-079-1

All rights reserved. No part of this publication may be reproduced, stored in a retrieval system, or transmitted in any form or by any means, electronic, mechanical, photocopying, recording or otherwise, without the prior permission of the publishers.

'I concluded that it was my task to be extraordinary ... a plaything ... to be used ... the fate of a special messenger. ... '

Søren Kierkegaard

Acknowledgements

It was in a lecture series in Edinburgh given by John Macmurray in the spring of 1954 that I first heard Kierkegaard mentioned.

It seems fitting that a last effort of mine to convey the content and import of this literary and philosophical innovator should be published in that same city.

In the years between I have been helped in this by many colleagues and good friends in the UK, the USA and Denmark.

Among them I would especially like to mention and thank Ted Honderich, without whose encouragement it would never have started, Bruce Kirmmse, for providing detailed historical material for the benefit of all Kierkegaard scholars, George Pattison for helping to keep the theology in focus, Edward Mooney, who with his poetic talent has so tellingly prised the still-living philosophical core from Kierkegaard's multi-genre writings, and Gordon Marino, whose gift for the idiom has brought Kierkegaard out of the pantheon and put him back on the streets.

Borre, 2022

Contents

Acknowledgements	*vii*
PREFACE	1
SUBJECTIVE THINKER	3
PHASE ONE: THE INDIRECT MESSAGES	10
PHASE TWO: THE DIRECT MESSAGES	22
PARTING SALVOES	34
BEHIND THE CATCHPHRASES	40
ISOLATION	71
MODEL MISFITS	80
DELIVERY DUES	84
THE DEALT HAND	94
TIMELY AFTERTHOUGHTS	99
Bibliography	*111*

Preface

What can a reader learn from the life of one who spent his own in a modest walled city in a comparatively small European state, with nothing but a handful of visits to Berlin to widen his horizon? A clue may be found in answers to another question: What was it that turned a young boy described by his headmaster as 'exceedingly childish and quite devoid of seriousness' into a literary and cultural celebrity?

That prompts a third: What drove a young man within a period of ten years to write twenty-eight works and enough entries in notebooks and journals to fill twelve thick volumes? Last, though far from least, why was he so obsessed with the individual?

We can learn as much from the reasons, motives and urges that drove Kierkegaard to writing as we can from the writing itself. We can both listen *to* and listen *for* the Kierkegaard who suspected that posterity would find the workings and worker as intriguing as the works. To many, he lies enigmatically behind a host of pseudonyms. However, given time, their separate identities emerge as a complex of motives driving this one individual to uncover what he tells us is needed for all to become their own and better selves.

Here we begin with the writings as any reader must, and without the 'impertinent questions' and 'learned dust' of biography that Friedrich Nietzsche not unwisely thought get in the way of an appreciation of great artists.[1] Yet Kierkegaard's art and his works are less easy to separate, so some detail will be pertinent along the way, indeed quite a lot. The origins, though, can wait until the work has had its say.

---

[1] See Friedrich Nietzsche, *Untimely Meditations*, ed. Daniel Breazeale, trans. R. J. Hollingdale, Cambridge, 1997, p. 97.

Subjective thinker

There are more Either/Or's in Kierkegaard than those facing the reader of the famous originally two volume publication of that name. The book itself includes several listed by the Either's protagonist who comes to the despairing conclusion that you will regret whichever alternative you choose: 'If you marry, you will regret it; if you do not marry, you will regret it'.[2] Of these particular alternatives more later, while to start here on the right foot, or on both feet, we take note of another oddly futile pair of alternatives, where the very fact that neither choice makes any difference provides a vital clue to something the author would have his every reader bear in mind.

It is found in a brief episode in an equally long book where the author, Johannes Climacus, his name borrowed from a seventh-century monk famous for his *Scala Paradisi* (or *Ladder of Divine Ascent* in its English version), imagines meeting the famous German Enlightenment writer, critic and philosopher G. E. Lessing. Impressed by this fleet-footed thinker's ability to escape the encapsulating of ideas of well-known thinkers made fashionable in Kierkegaard's time by G. W. F. Hegel, Johannes wonders how Lessing would have responded to having his work being similarly pickled or cured as that of an exemplary subjective thinker. Subjective thinking happens to be Johannes's topic. But subjective is subjective.

---

2   *Søren Kierkegaards Skrifter (SKS)*, Copenhagen, 1997–2013, 2, p. 47/ *Either/Or: A Fragment of Life*, trans. Alastair Hannay, London, 1992, p. 54

In that meeting with the great enlightener, two scenarios are imagined: in one Johannes rattles off the individual ideas to Lessing as the master's own and 'enfolds him obligingly in an admirer's embrace' as the 'one to whom he owed it all'. In the other, Lessing just happening to be within earshot, Johannes chatters excitedly over this 'matchless' discovery of his own. In the first scene, Lessing smilingly disengages himself, leaving Johannes, red-faced and 'an object of ridicule'; in the second, the great man, with an 'ambiguously admiring mien', thumps him on the shoulder and says: 'You're right about this, if only I'd known!'[3]

As a promoter of subjective thinking, Johannes would realize more quickly than anyone how this 'wily Odysseus' had 'got the better of him'.[4] Yet he, or his guiding hand, has shown himself here to be no less wily: by a subtle counterfactual twist, Lessing's support has been enlisted in something for which support is officially impossible. The prestigious example becomes the visibly vanishing point on which the spinning top of *Concluding Unscientific Postscript*'s seven hundred pages rotates. Naturally enough, as one who 'rests in himself', Lessing has no need of such 'companionship'.[5] But that the sheer mobility of his thought has kept it from the outstretched hands of the paragraph salters encourages Johannes to hope that what he is about to say may likewise evade the 'world historical' butchers' clutches.[6]

Was it a hope fulfilled? Kierkegaard is today the talk of many towns. Who hasn't heard of the 'leap of faith', or of the 'father of existentialism'? Does it matter

---

3 *SKS* 17, p. 72/*Concluding Unscientific Postscript* (*CambridgeUP*), trans. Alastair Hannay, Cambridge, 2009, p. 60.
4 Ibid.
5 *SKS* 17, p. 101/*CUP*, p. 87.
6 *SKS* 17, p. 104/*CUP*, p. 90.

that the former expression is nowhere to be found in Kierkegaard's works, or that this particular "*ism*" first appeared during World War II, almost a century after the writer's death? Perhaps not, the tabs help to locate a writer who we feel we should be able to talk about. A problem with such wrappings is that they reinforce a temptation to package authors' achievements in ways designed to aid our memories, by slotting them conveniently into capsules answering to the classificatory needs of compendia. The requirements of Readers are also to be met, with topics duly selected in line with the educational demands of student curricula. These enable students to 'place' writers and to reel off the names of others who have touched on the same themes, but permit only superficial access to their work. In this respect Kierkegaard's writings offer editors a wide choice of topics, from literary theory and aesthetics to pedagogy, innovative ethics, politics and the social order, as well as moral psychology, not to mention theology. We might imagine Kierkegaard appreciating the fact — so long as it is one — that subjective thinking is not a currently topical topic and has so far been left out of their pickings.

An article celebrating the bicentenary in 2013 of Kierkegaard's birth bore the title 'an octopus with long tentacles'.[7] The metaphor can be too apt: an octopus's tentacles (experts will tell us they are more accurately called 'arms') tap into a diverse world, but they also report back to more than one brain. However, in a human even one brain is enough to cause confusion. The varied feedback is registered in a centre and can present

---

7   Emil Nicklas Johnsen, 'Blekksprut med lange Tentakler. Om 200-åringen Søren Kierkegaards historie i Norge' [Octopus with Long Tentacles. On the 200-year-old Kierkegaard's History in Norway]', *Arr. Idéhistorisk tidsskrift*, no. 1 (2014).

itself there as a problem of coordination, whether in the form of a body of knowledge or in the now fashionable terms of the problematic 'identity' of its recipient. For Kierkegaard, the problem was one of how each of us might become a single self.

This topic was one that Kierkegaard later claimed also held not just his own self but his work together. In an assortment of genres from the pseudonymously published *Either/Or* to a personal onslaught on the church and its personnel twelve years later, he claimed it provided a continual thread from start to finish. Both the beginning and the end caused surprise: the first pseudonymous work with its genre-indifferent range of topics and scandalous 'Diary of a Seducer' and the personally conducted cannonade at the close. In between, there were several major works that made little impact at the time but in due course produced a flurry of conflicting comment.

Kierkegaard would later say that he had written himself into his writing, that his writing was what he became, that it had been his own 'development'[8] and 'upbringing'.[9] That can be true in several directions, one simply being that the occupation left him mentally and physically exhausted as well as, at the very end, penniless. But the effort that emptied him had also produced the extraordinarily complex yet focused writer we know.

---

8   *SKS* 21, NB10:192, p. 359/*Kierkegaard's Journals and Notebooks* (*KJN*), Copenhagen, vols. 1-11/2, 2007–2020, 5, p. 371* (preferred to the translation's 'education', although the context is one in which Kierkegaard also says that he has been 'pressed', time and again, into circumstances that made him write). The asterisk in this and future references denotes that the translation has been adjusted, sometimes only in respect of punctuation.

9   *SKS* 22, NB11:204, p.127*KJN* 16, pp. 124-125* (again, preferred to the translation's 'education' in so far as the latter can suggest the acquiring of knowledge, or manners, rather than personal growth).

Yet, then again, he would claim that the occupation that 'made him' — not, of course, in the sense of a celebrity, but as the person he became — was also one in which he could *escape* from being this self-in-the-making. Only when occupied in the writing in which he *became* himself was he able also to *forget* that self-making self. Yes, he admits that writing was therapy and quite possibly something he could neither do nor be without: a compulsion in other words, like a drug habit, just as those with less talent resort to narcotics in search of more or to forget that they have less. Talent, too, of course needs sustaining, lapses of creativity simply adding to the malady that writing may help one to forget. When drained, Kierkegaard was a 'steamship with an engine too large for the ship's construction',[10] but as long as the writing went well he could confide to his only life-long friend that he was 'afloat again' with the 'machinery' once more 'in full swing'.[11] Struggling with the many motives that moved his pen, Kierkegaard came to see for himself the parts they played and their significance for his aims to become and honour the single self, not just as his destiny but as that of each of us. So much so, he prophesied, that 'not only my writings but indeed my life, the intriguing secret of the whole machinery' will 'one day be studied ... '.[12]

A reason for doing so today is the thought that, at a time when it becomes clear that a divisive politics of identity and an inquisitorial 'cancel culture' are two sides of the same coin, those whose struggles force them ever more deeply into a face-to-face confrontation

---

10   *SKS* 20, JJ:375, p. 256/*KJN* 2, p. 245.
11   *SKS* 28, letter 88, p. 171, 15 May 1843 from Berlin/*Kierkegaard's Writings*, vol. 25, *Letters and Documents*, trans. Henrik Rosenmeier, Princeton, 1979, here my translation.
12   *SKS* 20, NB3:22, p. 256/*KJN* 4, p. 256.

with the human condition may be better qualified than others to pave a way towards a more generous and accommodating society. The quick dismissal of critics of those who demonstratively promote the causes of unfavoured groups may be too facile an approach. There may be reason to support another that says, as a protagonist in *Either/Or* surprisingly but challengingly suggests, that we are *all* exceptions.

Resentment and anger may then be returned from the cover of flag-waving crowds shouldering 'we' slogans, to a one-to-one 'neighbourly' context, where the 'I' anonymity of collective umbrellas are folded and people take personal responsibility for their actions and reactions or their failures to act or react.

It is not implausible, after all, that Kierkegaard's cultivation of his unusual beginnings in Denmark's Golden Age opened his eyes to what his writings could present as a deeper sense of human homelessness. His belief that he had seen what Christianity really means, its 'truth', took the form of a sense of single selfhood to be grasped in a self-awareness that is not the egotistical soul-searching so easily associated with a focus on the individual, but an honest self-appraisal at a level deep enough for the option of existential homelessness to be faced for what it is. By sweeping away the scenarios in which our lives blur the nakedness and isolation of the self-aware beings that we inherently are, Kierkegaard believed his own situation revealed to him what being an individual means for all, or each, of us.[13]

For the philosopher Ludwig Wittgenstein, Kierkegaard,

---

13   Some forms of expression used here are drawn from my 'Kierkegaard against the herd' in the Institute of Art and Ideas' online magazine <https://iai.tv/articles/kierkegaard-against-the-herd-auid-1826?auid=2020>.

apart from being a saint, was the 'most penetrating thinker of the nineteenth century'.[14] A Nordic novelist casts him as the devil[15] and an American philosopher sees in him an enemy of truth.[16] Fellow citizens doubted his sanity, as do some contemporary commentators, but among the conflicting descriptions this innovative writer has attracted is that of being 'the sanest man of his generation'.[17] To a globalizing but simultaneously disintegrating world, a writer able to provoke such widely divergent reactions may still have something to tell us.

---

14   Ludwig Wittgenstein, in correspondence with M. O'C Drury, *Acta Philosophical Fennica*, Amsterdam, 1976, vol. 28, pp. 1-2, 1976.
15   William Heinesen, *De fortapte Spillemenn* [The Doomed Fiddlers], Copenhagen, 1965, 144, my trans.
16   Walter Kaufmann, ed., *From Dostoevsky to Sartre*, New York 1956, p. 20.
17   George Price, *The Narrow Pass: A Study of Kierkegaard's Concept of Man*, New York, 1963, p. 11.

Phase One: The indirect messages

There are several possible beginnings, but here we skip over a few and start with a visit to Berlin in the autumn of 1841. It was on a five-month first stay there that Søren Kierkegaard, now twenty-eight years old, began a ten-year spell of almost uninterrupted 'productivity'. The decade would see twenty-eight works both large and slim, as well as entries in notebooks and journals enough to fill twelve volumes in English translation (with commentary included). Ten of the works were published under pseudonyms, yet often on or near the same date there appeared others under Kierkegaard's own name. These were labelled 'Edifying Discourses', and later 'Christian Discourses'. They took lines from scripture to spell out in clear terms their implications for how it says we should lead our lives. The pseudonymous works, however, began at ground level, opening up life's challenges from a wide range of perspectives from whose changing foci various levels of response are portrayed. The mode of communication here is said by the one pseudonym who is seemingly in charge to be 'indirect' in a way to be made clearer below. There emerges a gradual classification between aesthetic, ethical and religious responses, each with its own internal ascending scale.

The first pseudonymous work, written largely in Berlin although parts later included had already been written earlier, made Kierkegaard famous overnight in Denmark and not long after throughout Scandinavia. On its appearance in 1843, *Either/Or* (*Enten/Eller*) excited many young writers. The first part included 'The Diary of a Seducer' and provoked a scandal in Denmark. The literary elite was (or made sure to appear) scandalized, while young radicals took immediately to the work. Its opening aphorisms, expressing ennui, cynicism and a tired disillusionment, along with reflections on Mozart's operas and tragedy, were in tune with new both literary and political developments. We will come to *Either/Or*'s second part later.

Further pseudonymous works immediately followed. *Repetition* (*Gjentagelsen*) is a novella in the form of a wiser man's correspondence with a much younger man that he never meets, but who has difficulties over a love affair. Its theme is the regaining of one's lost world, not by looking back (and being helped by philosophy) but forward in seeking some new way of conceiving it. If our world is to be one that we are at home in, we must hope that *it*, that is to say our world not *the* world, comes up with what that takes, for we have no instruments to achieve it all on our own.

According to *The Concept of Anxiety* (*Begrebet Angest*), this world of ours is replete with snares of the kind that Eve is said to have encountered in the Garden of Eden. They are symbolized by that 'fall' but are, in actuality, situations that are so much an ingrown feature of life that we have little or no ability or to see them for what they are. By making humankind blind to its inherent spirituality, the blind habits of millennia have anaesthetized us from the real trials of spirit. To prevent seeing too deeply or clearly into life's enigma, we lean on 'what is done' and cultivate the familiar. The author uses vertigo as a metaphor for the one whose 'eye' happens to look down into the 'yawning abyss'. The anxiety of the book's title is a 'dizziness of freedom that emerges when spirit looks down into its own possibilities and grabs hold of finiteness to support itself'.[18]

We read, too, of the 'fateful conflict' of that 'glance' or 'moment' (*Øieblik*) in time when the moment is 'touched by eternity'.[19] The topic is taken up in a book published in the same month as *Anxiety*. In *Philosophical Crumbs* (*Philosophiske Smuler*) we find some tightly woven speculation on what the reader would haxve to believe if the 'paradox' of time merging with the eternal, or vice versa, were true. We are also told that the eternal can be grasped only transiently, in the moment of receiving it from the 'teacher', and that, for this reason, it is the teacher we must first have faith in, not what is taught as though something we can personally catch hold of and take home with us.[20] What we are to believe in faith is not doctrine, something to pick up or a set of rules to follow, which then place us in or on the way to the truth, but a link of some kind that we actively maintain with the teacher himself.

In that same June month of 1844, Kierkegaard published an approximately sixty-page collection of eight detached prefaces (*Forord*), to which the author-editor, Nicolaus Notabene, supplies his own. The targets are mainly local in the form of reactions to reviews of Kierkegaard's works to date. But the collection also includes material that, due to their local references, has been omitted from these works. The tone, as we would expect, is light and irony evident throughout. The final preface has the author concluding that, having made

---

18 SKS 4, p. 365/ *The Concept of Anxiety*, trans. Alastair Hannay, New York, 2014, p. 75.
19 SKS 4, p. 390/ *The Concept of Anxiety*, p. 107.
20 SKS 4, p. 264/*Philosophical Crumbs* (in *Repetition and Philosophical Crumbs*), trans. M. G. Piety, Oxford 2009, p. 131.

many attempts at a philosophical explanation of life, he finds that he can get along quite nicely without.

In the previous year, along with *Repetition* and only five months after *Either/Or*, another now familiarly titled book appeared. *Fear and Trembling* (*Frygt og Bæven*) develops a theme touched on almost casually at the very end of the second of two large sections of *Either/Or*, these forming the major part of its second half, the Or. A hint is dropped there that a social outcast need not be a loser but, in the pain and despair of failure to associate, may find a deeper meaning in what it means to 'realize the universal'. It requires of reluctant exceptions, those who are unwillingly outside, that they forge their *individual* relationships to the universal and commonalty, that is to say, to what people can be seen to have and do for each other in common. To do so, calls for an inversion of the general ('universal') assumption, also embodied in language, namely that the universal or the concept comes before the individual or the particular instance. We are to be more than just examples, and must come to acknowledge that in life the particular is superior to the universal. It means that dropouts may have an opportunity to forge a better relationship to the universal than if they somehow managed to *re*-identify themselves as members of a society where individuals define themselves by their relationship to the universal in social roles, or any other kind of collective for that matter, including those offering misfits conveniently *anti*-social roles. The reader is briefly offered the possibility of exceptionality in some 'nobler sense' than that of the superior, vain, defiant, revengeful, indifferent or self-pitying outsider.[21]

The example of an exception profiled soon after in *Fear and Trembling* is not readily grasped as a case of such nobility. The centrepiece here is Abraham obeying

---

21   *SKS* 3, p. 313/ *Either/Or*, trans. Alastair Hannay, London 1992, p. 589.

God's command to sacrifice his son Isaac as proof of his faith. However scriptural, the scenario as presented in the book is more easily associated with the subculture of gang membership and blind obedience than with faith in any conventionally religious sense. However, the seemingly wide-eyed pseudonymous author invites the reader to accept as a premise a tradition that has for millennia praised Abraham for his unerring trust and dubbed him the 'Father of Faith'.[22]

The mood of the book's first part is that of wide-eyed amazement at Abraham's fortitude. Sharing the narrator's sense of wonder of someone who as a child was told the 'beautiful tale of how God tried Abraham', but who as he grew older understood it 'less and less', and with the 'shudder of thought' now upstaging the seduction of the story's aesthetic appeal,[23] we are to imagine the father's own thoughts as he climbed the mountain to perform the sacrifice. He does so silently, for nothing he might truthfully say will explain, either to us or to his son, what it is that he intends to do. The alternative would be to lie, but Abraham is a good man. The author's name, by the way, is Johannes *de silentio*.

The second part offers the reader something like three logical demonstrations aimed at those who find *reason* to praise Abraham, rather than doing so from habit or hearsay. These include the German philosopher G. W. F. Hegel,[24] whose name appears strategically eight times in the three 'problemata' (or conundrums), in which the reader is given the options of siding with Abraham and having to declare the particular to be superior to the universal, or of continuing to believe the conventional

---
22 *SKS* 4, p. 115/*Fear and Trembling*, trans. Alastair Hannay, London, 1985, p. 52.
23 Ibid., 105/p. 44.
24 *SKS* 4, p. 160 /*Fear and Trembling*, p. 96.

opposite and being forced to call him a criminal or lunatic. From this, Kierkegaard's literate readers would understand that *Fear and Trembling* is essentially a missile aimed at the still influential Hegelian tradition with its program of reaching the Absolute by way of the Mind, or Concept, a project that assumes from the start the superiority of the universal over the particular. The reader is invited to conclude that any praise due to Abraham can be justified only by admitting the reverse. Only by accepting the 'paradox that the single individual, as particular, stands in an absolute relation to the absolute' can Abraham be saved.[25]

Kierkegaard believed *Fear and Trembling* would be the one book to 'immortalize [his] name as an author'. It would be read in 'different languages'.[26] In the course of time, several other works came to enjoy that status. One of these has already been quoted, Johannes Climacus's massive *Concluding Unscientific Postscript to the Philosophical Crumbs* (*Afsluttende uvidenskabelig Efterskrift til de philosophiske Smuler*). Its subtitle describes it as a 'Mimic, Pathetic, Dialectic Compilation' and 'Existential Contribution'. The work is now counted as a classic of existentialist literature.

The pseudonymous author calls himself a humourist, something that caused initial (and some persisting) confusion. To correct the wrong impression that this title had given to his readers, Kierkegaard later declared that the comical aspects were exactly those in which the 'earnestness' of *Postscript*'s appeal to the individual was to be found. Readers taken in by the familiar Aristotelian and Hegelian conceptual apparatus of the time adopted by Johannes Climacus, had tried to construct 'individual

---

25 *SKS* 4, p. 207/*Fear and Trembling*, p. 144.
26 *SKS* 22, NB12, p.147/*KJN* 6, p. 237.

theses and transpose them into a dialectical mode', while what the book is introducing, and wherein lies its novelty, is 'personality'.[27]

This word had a special meaning in Kierkegaard's time. It was used in a radical and progressive religious sense to denote the 'new person'. For some, this new person was to be found in historical figures, or public-spirited personalities in today's sense though with clear religious overtones. These were people who lent their shoulders visibly and even noisily to the completion of God's plan for humankind. Notable among those who took 'personality' in this both visible and vocal sense in Denmark were supporters of the educationist and historian N. F. S. Grundtvig. They included Kierkegaard's own older brother Peter Christian, who later became a bishop. The opening pages of *Postscript* deal briskly with this newsworthy notion of personality:

> *Having Grundtvig on one's side is something no one could wish who wants to know definitely where one is, and who does not wish to be where there is a hubbub, especially when the location of the hubbub is the only more specific determination of where one is.*[28]

Postscript's own view is that the new person avoids noise and excitement, and has absolutely no interest in achieving historical significance. The goal of the itinerary presented in that work is an ever-present one: the here and now of becoming one's better self, the 'singular self' with its location plotted, not in a moving historical landscape for all to see and applaud, but in the

---

27   *SKS* 22, NB13:61, p. 310/*KJN* 6, pp. 312-313*. The translation has misleadingly 'a personality'.
28   *SKS* 7, p. 51/*CUP*, p. 40.

privacy of a relation to an absolute that can in principle be shared with everyone and by anyone.

It is clear that Johannes Climacus, also the author of the earlier and very differently compact *Philosophical Crumbs*, has not intended the work, as commentators still sometimes claim, as a parody of Hegelians, or a long-drawn-out joke at their expense. Its aim, rather, seems to be to jostle and nudge readers in this way and that, so that they themselves begin to see spiritual possibilities that both the intellectuals and convention are, for reasons open to psychological insight, preventing them from seeing. The humorous exterior and 'unscientific' — or more accurately 'unscholarly' — mixture of treatise, anecdote, and satire provides here a wide-ranging literary entertainment with a deadly serious purpose. How it intends to achieve it becomes clear. Towards the end, to the still alert readers' surprise if not dismay or disgust, the author signs off by saying that he takes it all back.

Is this just another joke? It seems not. Rather, it is an indication of *Postscript*'s intention and the method that this calls for. The 'task' is a Socratic one. In his many encounters with people who tended to make opinion sound like dogma, that 'gadfly' street philosopher in Greece claimed to *know* nothing. His role, as he saw it, was that of getting others to generate their own convictions by being offered clues or associations that helped an already established though long-forgotten and somehow innate truth, to be jolted back into memory. It was a mental form of midwifery that became known as 'maieutic'.

It is here that we see how these pseudonymous 'messages' are not 'direct communications', or even messages in the ordinary sense at all, or strings of words saying something that we want to tell others or to be told, for instance about the weather or the latest ware casualties. In order for these 'indirect' communications to come off, something has to be contributed by the recipient; not, however, in the form of something that the recipient already has on offer to give, but in a new appreciation or admission of something that the recipient hitherto lacks but can come upon.

Unlike Socrates, whose approach assumed *mimesis*, or the prior establishment of a truth that can be recovered by strategic prompting, for Johannes Climacus truth accordingly is not something to be recovered as though from a blueprint erased by time from our collective memories and recoverable by skilful prompting. This pseudonym is 'existentialist' enough, in a sense to be discussed later, to see truth as shaped only in the future and in the form of increasing and individual awareness of the scope of our possibilities in the light of what we can come to recognize in ourselves as our shortcomings.

The surprising revocation aims in this way to secure a readership freed from any idea that what it has been reading up to that point is doctrine; or that it has any authority other than that which a reader's own sensitivities may give to it. Nor is it assumed that the author's background has given him any special access to truths. That has already been made clear in the introduction where, to 'avoid confusion' on this matter, he says,

> I, Johannes Climacus, born in this city and now thirty years old, a quite ordinary human being just like anyone else, assume that for me, as much as for a serving maid and a professor, there awaits a highest good called an eternal happiness. I have heard that Christianity is to provide one with that good. And now I ask how do I enter into relation with this doctrine.[29]

---

29 *SKS* 7, pp. 24-25/*CUP*, p. 16.

By the end, we realize that our relation to this highest good is not to that of following a doctrine and that, since in this respect we are all quite ordinary human beings, it is the same for everyone. Accepting the Christian offer, as *Postscript* presents it, is an entirely personal choice to follow an example whose credentials as contractor for that good are taken against both our natural and intellectual inclinations and in isolation. Unless you can see yourself in the text in that light, you should put the book back on the shelf.

Not unexpectedly, Kierkegaard's unorthodox works invited both misinterpretation and bewilderment. In the case of a large work published a year previously, *Stages on Life's Way*, such incomprehension is understandable. With its subtitle *Studies by Various People, Collected, Prepared for the Press and Published by Hilarius Bogbinder* (*Stadier paa Livets Vei, Studier af Forskjellige, Sammenbragte, befordrede til Trykken og udgivne af Hilarius Bogbinder*), this more than four-hundred-and-fifty-page sequel to *Either/Or* contained new perspectives that readers will not have appreciated as the real author must have hoped. That its *dramatis personae* include both *Either/Or*'s pseudonymous editor Victor Eremita and the Seducer who had then been under his editorship, suggests a wider view from higher up or else further along. A new pseudonym, Frater Taciturnus (Silent Brother), signs the book's main contribution and also writes a letter to the reader. That it is not addressed to another contributor seems even more clearly than *Postscript*'s revocation to indicate that it is the individual reader who is the intended recipient.

What may still be unclear is the identity of the sender. Could it be that here we have real author appearing more openly on the pages?

Stages was published just nine months before *Postscript*[30] and was as poorly received as the latter would be. According to Kierkegaard *Postscript*, although the 'keystone of an earlier authorial endeavour on a grand scale, 'sold sixty copies and 'received no mention anywhere'.[31] If the earlier *Stages* was seen as a sequel to *Either/Or*, the disinterest would be understandable. Those with their memory of *Either/Or* still intact would have in mind its first part (on first publication a separate volume), with the irony and bitterness of its aphorisms, its satire and the infamous 'Diary'. This new and seemingly haphazard 'compilation' of novels, essays and papers was invested with a more explicit and 'existential' rendering of the aesthetic, ethical and religious stages, while these were still awaiting their ordered arrangement and conceptual definitions in *Postscript*, along with their contextualization there within a development traced in the previous pseudonymous works up to and including *Stages*.

There is, however, a further explanation for the initial or even sheer disorganization of *Stages*. It is that, even with or because of its wider-angled discussions, the book has a correspondingly narrower yet thereby clearer focus on the real author's personal and still private reasons for taking up his pen. Its subtitle, 'A Story of Suffering, Psychological Experiment' is also revealing and it is symptomatic that the largest and final section is scripted by Frater Taciturnus, a pseudonym Kierkegaard would assume as a cover for himself, and that its title is ' "Guilty?" — "Not-Guilty?" '. The background for this new Either/Or is found in a comment Kierkegaard made

---

30 See *SKS* 22, NB13:55, p. 309/*KJN* 6, p. 311.
31 *Papers and Journals: A Selection*, trans. Alastair Hannay, London, 1996, p. 436.

when once more though more briefly in Berlin and making his first sketches for *Stages*. He had written:

> Had I had faith I would have stayed with Regine. Praise be to God, I have now understood it. I have been on the point of losing my mind these days. [Humanly] speaking I have done the right thing for her, but perhaps I should never have become engaged.[32]

It was just one month after breaking off his one-year engagement to Regine Olsen that Kierkegaard had left Copenhagen for that first visit to Berlin.

---

32 *SKS* 18, JJ:115, 7 May 1843, p. 177/*KJN* 2, p. 164.

Phase Two: The direct messages

Frustrated by the lukewarm response to his recent works and unhappy that they had not made a greater stir, Kierkegaard under the Frater Taciturnus pseudonym, which of course fooled no one, then took up his pen and provoked a satirical journal (the *Corsair*, whose editor, like the young radicals, tended to take his side) into giving him some humorous publicity. It had done so with other local celebrities, so why should *he*, in this case if somewhat ironically, be an exception?

The result of the public's reaction to the *Corsair*'s lampooning was that Kierkegaard could not be seen on the streets without being mocked by callow youths for his general appearance and attire, both of which were repeatedly caricatured by the journal's illustrator. Forced to stay indoors, and losing the support of hitherto sympathetic readers, colleagues and even helpers, which also meant losing the discreet protection of pseudonyms that kept real authors' names out of discussion surrounding their work, Kierkegaard was now fair game for critics and public alike.

Lockdown merely sharpened his pen. It also meant that he could be more open with and to himself and thereby, in the privacy of his journals, to us. There would be more to write about too: the experience itself, his own reactions and reactions to those reactions and those of others, but not least his own literary career and its motivation.

Cultural historians like to separate creative artists' work into periods. There are the early, middle and late Beethoven, early and late Goethe, and artists such as Picasso and Willem de Kooning with their periods of anomaly, the one early and the other late. Kierkegaard's career can also be divided into an early period of the early pseudonyms, with their many-voiced proponents with several things to say on a variety of topics and points of view, all of it apparently screening the real author's personal identity; a second period as the notorious social critic hiding from the world, but a well-known public figure all the same and with a provocative agenda; and finally, a sudden, quite unexpected period in which an apparently severely religious author engaged in a savage one-man rebellion against the church.

This is too simple or elliptical a view. By reaching back to a time preceding the events that brought guilt into the picture, we find a germ from which all three so-called periods grow in what can be seen as an ironclad consistency. By including its existential or psychological context, the consistency might even be called logical.

In the summer of 1835, just one year after Kierkegaard's mother had died, and with several siblings having preceded her, his father detected signs of a nervous breakdown in the younger son. The twenty-two-year-old was sent on a recreational summer holiday in north Sjælland (Zealand). In its coastal landscape with woods and lanes and a well-known lake, all described in telling detail by Kierkegaard in what can be read as experimental literary landscaping, it became a time of reflection. The diaries from there speak of the 'few dear departed ones',[33] and it is from here that we have a now familiar quotation about 'find[ing] the idea for which I

---

[33] *SKS* 17, AA:6, p. 14/*KJN* 1, p. 9.

am willing to live and die'.[34] The young man was longing for a 'truth' that he could call his 'own', something other than the impersonal truths of knowledge and science, for '[w]hat use would it be if truth were to stand there before me, cold and naked, not caring whether I acknowledged it or not ... inducing an anxious shiver rather than trusting devotion?'[35]

Having imagined his soul, he now thought mistakenly, as being somehow enclosed 'in a box' with a lock which, by 'pressing the spring', only something or someone outside could open, he now sees that 'before knowing anything else ... one must learn to know oneself '. Not wanting to 'decide the externals first and the fundamental afterwards', it is the 'Kingdom of Heaven' he thinks he should seek first. Having, as a student, looked in vain for a 'focal point on which all radii converge',[36] and on lamenting the dear departed just a few days previously, had envied the good fortune of one who finds an 'Archimedean point outside the constraints of time and space ... from which he could lift the whole world'.[37]

Disoriented and in a state of mental disarray, after seven years as a student the young Kierkegaard was in search of his 'I'.[38] In other words, he was undergoing what we today call an identity crisis. The solution was to ask the 'Deity'[39] to give him something useful to do. It would be a way towards self-realization, a task to undertake that would be both *his* but also the *truth*.

Readers of the pseudonyms and discourses up to *Postscript* will realize that Kierkegaard believed that

---

34 *SKS* 17, AA:12, p. 24/*KJN* 1, p. 19, emphasis removed.
35 Ibid.
36 *SKS* 17, AA:12, p. 27 /*KJN*, p. 22.
37 *SKS* 17, AA:6, p. 15/*KJN* 1, p. 10.
38 *SKS*.17, AA:12, pp. 27 and 30/*KJN* 1, pp. 21 and 24.
39 *SKS* I7, AA:1, p. 24/*KJN* 1, p. 19.

he had found such a task: it was to seek justification of the status of the individual: the exception to the rule in the scheme of things. Both this task and its trajectory had been given to him in meeting a sympathetic and intelligent young lady who, for quite personal reasons that caused him much inner conflict, he found he must betray. By breaching the promise that he had made through their one-year engagement, he had at that time also broken a vow made to society.

The solution to his own crisis that Kierkegaard sought was therefore not, as typically in our day, to find membership in a collective, whether subcultural, dissident or just private; it was to focus on something 'eternal', or 'absolute', that drew the focus away from association altogether and focused on a relation to God or, as a later pseudonym would put it, on 'something else', this something being the 'power' that 'established' it.[40]

This was not a deity of the kind that people generally appeal to, one that they can call on for help to change the world just for them, or one that they dutifully but also prudently as well as thankfully sing praises to when things go well. *Postscript* even says, to some readers shockingly, that God 'does not exist'.

That has to be understood. It doesn't mean that there is no God, but that God is not to be found in his Creation, whether as Idealists conceive this in their minds, or in the working out of a divine intention to be seen or deciphered in history. To 'exist' is to be 'constrained' by space and time: it is our human confinement. We who exist do so within the parameters of past, present and future, in other words 'change'. God, as Kierkegaard later writes, is 'unchangeable'.[41]

That, from a common point of view, may seem a defect,

---

40   *SKS* 11, p. 130/*The Sickness unto Death*, trans. Alastair Hannay, London, 1989, p. 44.
41   *SKS* 13, p. 321, *Guds Uforanderlighed*, Copenhagen, 1955. A sermon preached in May 1851, trans. David F. Swenson, Princeton, 1944.

even a blot on the escutcheon of divine omnipotence itself and God's assumed perfection. Surely God the Creator can do anything. But when understood in Kierkegaardian terms, it is a notion of perfection presented to ourselves, though as one we can never do more than approximate even if, according to Christianity, it is our destiny to aim at it, the alternative being despair. As Kierkegaard once wrote, to pray to God is not to try to bend the divine will or have God make any change; it is for oneself to be changed in the praying.[42]

Twelve years on from that summer break, in self-induced lockdown, Kierkegaard was now in a new state of anxiety. Alone, he was wondering whether in engaging in this task he had merely been bolstering his own ego, just doing something he liked doing, and in doing so stitching together a self that he could be proud of. These signed and pseudonymous works still pouring from his pen were undoubtedly in a sense 'his', but were they also 'truth'? And then there was all this criticism that he was making of his fellow citizens: was he perhaps unjustly exaggerating the demands made on the faithful by Christianity, speaking down to them while speciously claiming superiority for himself as an exemplary Christian? Was he in fact just a vain outsider and not one of the nobler kind? In short, had he, Søren Kierkegaard, any right to assume that what he had longed for on that summer day, had in fact been given to him; or had he been making a self after his own projected self-image? The theme would appear in another work, *The Sickness unto Death*.

It was in a turmoil of this inner kind, aggravated by external circumstances (moving to a series of apartments, a war that left him without his helper and

---

42   SKS 8, p. 137/*Upbuilding Discourses in Various Spirits*, trans. Howard V. Hong and Edna H. Hong, Princeton, 1993, p. 22.

himself in financial difficulties), that the later works were conceived and eventually published.

Three works are seminal. The non-pseudonymous *Works of Love* (*Kjerlighedens Gjerninger*) (1847) focuses on 'love of one's neighbour'. It tells us something we all know, that the neighbour may be anyone, but adds that real love of the neighbour contains no element of personal inclination other than a wish to promote love *in* the neighbour. 'Neighbour' refers to anyone within what might be called our moral scope or within moral distance, that is to say, those to whom you or I have some control over and responsibility regarding *how* it goes with them. It might be the next-door neighbour, but also an enemy you find taking shelter in a foxhole or shell-crater you yourself have just jumped into, as in Erich Maria Remarques' *All Quiet on the Western Front* from the First World War. A 'work' of love is active and with no element of passivity, that is to say, of whatever personal appeal something or someone has to you, even if you have it. Any such element is 'self-love', and even though it is found in practically everything we normally and 'naturally' and in a generally acceptable way call 'love', it is not that part of it that is love of the other. Love of others that is sought or received in any sense for ourselves is 'not consciously grounded in the eternal ... it can be changed'. It is '[o]nly when it is a duty to love ... [that] love is eternally secure against every change ... eternally emancipated in blessed independence'.[43] These thoughts are presented in a series of 'Christian deliberations in the form of discourse'.

It is in *The Sickness unto Death* (*Sygdommen til Døden*) (1849) that we read of the self as having been

---

43 *SKS* 9, p. 36/*Works of Love*, trans. Howard V. Hong and Edna H. Hong, Princeton, 1998, p. 34.

'established by something else'.[44] Its author, who is a Christian 'to an extraordinary degree',[45] is named 'Anti-Climacus'. He offers an 'exposition', or 'laying out', in other words something between 'edifying' literature and 'treatise' but in fact a mixture of both.[46] The matter laid out is despair. This we usually assume to be something we suffer when 'things' get the better of us. But if we think carefully, despair and desperation are not the same. When, in danger of drowning, you reach 'desperately' or 'in desperation' for the rope or lifebelt thrown to you, still hoping to grab hold of it and save your skin. But if the tide carries you ever further away, you 'despair' of reaching it. To despair is to *lose* hope or it is to have lost it. But then *The Sickness unto Death* tells us that despair is not a matter of the *world* getting the better of us: it is we ourselves who give up the struggle. The rope thrown to us, you might say, is the Christian idea that the eternal has entered time to save us (from 'error'), although the connection with Christianity is not made explicit until the book's second part. Two kinds of despair are diagnosed, and these then sub-divided. The first is a despairing 'not-yet' self that holds its spiritual possibilities at a distance, but with increasingly conscious ways of doing so as they come threateningly into view. Some of these may look like the opposite of despair, a blissful forgetting or forced gaiety, but it never quite works. The second kind of despair is a preference for one's own image of selfhood: instead of 'grounding [it]self transparently in the power that established it',[47] this self does its own grounding according to its own preferred image. It is a development that ends with

---

44   *SKS* 11, p. 130 / *The Sickness unto Death*, p. 44.
45   *SKS* 22, NB11:204, p. 128/*KJN* 6, p. 125.
46   *SKS* 11, p. 117 / *The Sickness unto Death*, p. 35.
47   *SKS* 11, p. 130/ *The Sickness unto Death*, p. 44.

thinking on the lines: if one is not this self, then one is nothing at all. Facing that alternative, of being nothing except what we find ourselves being, is in a sense where we should nevertheless begin, taking on responsibility for the possibilities that we are born with and seeing them in the light of that 'power' that grounded us with these possibilities. Finally, as we read in the last pages, to have first sensed that there is such a 'power', but to then turn one's back on it and 'declaring Christianity to be an untruth', is to 'sin against the Holy Ghost'. The 'formula' for being rid of this despair is phrased like this: '[I]n wanting to be itself, the self is grounded transparently in the power which established it'. This is the 'definition of faith'.[48]

Then there is the pseudonymous *Practice in Christianity* (1850) (*Indøvelse i Christendom*) in its three divisions. The first calls for 'awakening and inward deepening', the second 'expounds' relevant parts of the Bible and defines a sense of 'offence' (or what goes against the grain of natural aspiration) that is inseparable from faith, while the third stresses the extent of the demands made by Christianity. In the Preface, the Editor, Kierkegaard now in person, says that the 'pseudonymous author is here 'forc[ing] up the requirement for being a Christian to a supreme ideality'.[49] The message to readers is that to be Christians they should imitate Christ. That would include the suffering, but what, we ask, about crucifixion? Must Christians go that far? Clearly not: Christ *is* the truth, and to be a martyr you have to be counted as a witness to it.[50] Such witnesses are very few and traditionally confined to the group known as apostles. Kierkegaard

---

48 S*KS* 11, p. 242/*The Sickness unto Death*, p. 165.
49 S*KS* 12, p. 15/*Practice in Christianity*, trans. Howard V. Hong and Edna H. Hong, Princeton,1991, p. xv.
50 *SKS* 21, NB10:41, p. 278/*KJN* 5, p. 289.

can nevertheless, in a journal entry, talk of himself as 'laughter's martyr'. It is a kind of crucifixion, but if a martyrdom, then one that *he* had chosen.[51] He writes, in another entry, that this is a book of great importance to him personally. He calls it a potent remedy, but then adds tellingly that he himself might be one of the *few* who need it.[52]

The remark is crucial. We can well understand that a God as transcendent as that described in the pages of *Postscript* could take earthly form only in the figure of an exception or outsider. In his previous work, the *Crumbs*, its author has already remarked that the idea of the eternal entering leaves our understanding in pieces, so that all we can grasp of God is that he is our opposite, and that 'absolute difference cannot even be thought'.[53] God and Man differ absolutely, and Kierkegaard, who was at this time concluding his own 'missionary' work on behalf of Christianity in the context of what he referred to disparagingly as Christendom (*Christenhed*), makes advocacy of the imitation of Christ sound like a clear expression of his *own* outsider's stance. Any actual imitation of Christ will always be a passport to social exile and would, if taken quite literally, imply mass suicide. We are led to ponder over whether a less isolated Kierkegaard might have been content with urging his reader to follow Christ's words rather than example.

That Kierkegaard handed a personal copy of *Practice* to the Danish primate might strike some as a sign that he had lost his bearings. Bishop Mynster would be the first to see that its burden was that he no longer had a job. When what count are works and not words, foot

---

51   SKS 21, NB10:42, p. 279/*KJN* 5, p. 289.
52   SKS 22, NB11:204, p. 127 *KJN* 16, pp. 124-125.
53   SKS 4, p. 249/*Philosophical Crumbs*, p. 117.

soldiers armed with the rulebook of Christ's example make staff officers behind the lines redundant. *Practice* puts the whole church in question and at that time Mynster *was* the church.

But this was not as wrongheaded as it can seem. There were at least two reasons why Kierkegaard could look on Mynster as a vital factor in his cause. The bishop might see that he himself was among those chosen few whose wealth of experience made them eligible for the remedy. If he did, then he might join forces with Kierkegaard in a gradual process of reformation that would bring the church closer to the New Testament. There had also been a long-standing family connection. The once up-and-coming young pastor had been Kierkegaard's father's choice for his family's Sunday worship, and, as the priest in the Church of Our Lady, Mynster had officiated at the fourteen-year-old's confirmation. In later years, he was the one church official that Kierkegaard respected and could go to for and receive understanding. If only in private, Mynster might express encouragement.

There was something else, too, although it pointed in the opposite direction. Exhausted and frustrated by a lack of response to his latest work, Kierkegaard could see his writing career coming to an end. Paradoxically, given the message of *The Sickness unto Death*, his own despair was not to defy Christianity but to dream of retirement in a country parish where he could preach without isolating himself by antagonizing people. As late as 1849 Kierkegaard admitted that 'an appointment in a small rural parish' had always been at the back of his mind.[54] Here, too, Mynster might help him. At one point, no doubt not just out of sympathy, the bishop even advised Kierkegaard to do that.[55]

---

54   *SKS* 21, NB10:60, p. 289 / *KJN* 5, p. 300.
55   *SKS*. 20, NB:57, p. 52/ *KJN* 4, p. 50.

It was, in any case, a time for looking back and reflecting on why he had become a writer, the writer we know. He confided his own views on this to himself, and to us, in a journal entry dated April the 19th, 1848, a bad year both for him and for Denmark: it was the start of the First Schleswig War.

He wrote that it was 'essentially because of her [Regine]', his 'melancholia', and his 'money' that he had become a writer. That he had loved Regine 'nothing [was] more certain'. But she had been unable to break the silence of his melancholia. Regarding the money, his father had predicted that he would 'drink and dream it away', when what it had actually done was give him an opportunity to develop 'all the torment of self-torture in [his] heart'.

That sounds, though not convincingly, as if he would have preferred poverty and a steady job. Yet he writes, now in hope and not despair, that with God's help he will become himself. With a new-found faith in 'Christ's assistance' (this being the time of *Practice in Christianity*), he could overcome his melancholia. That, too, he says was something he had 'loved', it being through it that he had loved the 'world'. But all of this had gone to raising the tension: her 'suffering', his 'exertion', and then at last, 'living with mockery'. Now, having also for financial reasons to look after his own future, he would — it seems thankfully — take on a job. And what job? He would 'become a priest'.[56]

This moment, however brief, was certainly not the one in which eternity meets time. In sheer exhaustion, sensing the futility of his mission, Kierkegaard was on the point of giving up. It was not long, however, before the inveterate polemicist was in action once more and generating enough steam in that over-dimensioned

---

56   *SKS* 20, NB4:152, p. 57/*KJN* 4, p. 357.

machinery once more for the ship to gather headway and come back on course. Seven years later he would be calling the priest, among other far more uncomplimentary things, 'that incarnation of nonsense wrapped in long clothes'.⁵⁷

---

57 SKS 13, *Øieblikket*, no. 5, July 27, 1855/ *The Moment and Later Writings*, pp. 157-158/ *KW* XXIII, p. 39.

Parting salvoes

Caught up in his portrayal of the 'truth' of Christianity, Kierkegaard admitted that he once came close to putting himself into the portrait, even confessing to having for a moment actually done so. It had been as though *he* had been the truth simply by having presented it in compelling prose, or 'poetizing' as he calls it, but also having endured enough misery to be able to call it 'sacrifice'. In that moment, he 'seemed to understand that the world, or Denmark, needed a martyr'. He had been ready 'by laying down [his] life' to back up his writing 'in the most decisive manner'.[58]

Seeing that he believed he was about to die anyway from sheer fatigue, there was some disingenuousness in this if not also vanity and maybe desperation. But the light had dawned. He writes that even though his fate was a 'sad one', all this talk of martyrdom had just been a matter of 'hypochondria'.[59] Well aware that he himself was far from living up to the ideal, he was the 'unhappy lover' whose unhappiness had made him into a poet and (in *Either/Or*) 'the most inspired champion of marriage'. That was his first mission. Lacking the strength to be a 'witness to the truth', for which he could be put to death, he was born to be someone who as 'poet' and 'thinker' could be 'sacrificed in a lesser sense'.[60]

---

58 *SKS* 21, NB10:200, p. 367/*KJN* 5, p. 378.
59 *SKS* 22, NB11:20, p. 18/*KJN* 6, p. 14.
60 *SKS* 21, NB10:200, pp. 368-369/ *KJN* 5, p. 379.

If Kierkegaard was not a witness to the truth, then Bishop Mynster was decidedly not that either. But on the respected primate's death in January 1854, and in an address at the ceremonial memorial service on the 5th of February 1854, this was just what his successor eloquently hailed him as being. That the new primate was Hans Lassen Martensen, Kierkegaard's gifted and long-standing, career-tracking and Hegel-inspired *bête-noir*, undoubtedly added urgency to the polemical pen. It immediately produced 'Was Bishop Mynster a "Witness for the Truth," One of the "Proper Witnesses to the Truth" — Is *This the Truth?*'.

The article was ready for publication by the end of February 1854, the very month in which Mynster died, but it did not appear in the newspaper *Fædrelandet* until the end of December. Why? Was this almost year-long delay due to respect for the dead, or perhaps for all those still living who revered the man and his life? Or were there those doubts again about a 'poet' having a right to criticize others?

The real reason seems to have been politics, not Kierkegaard's own involvement but a concern not to have political squabbles about succession to the primacy blur the profile of his own cause. Strong forces favoured a national liberal candidate and Kierkegaard, for whom undermining the establishment was never high on the agenda, could have been seen to be actually participating in the campaign for the conservative Martinsen's appointment. There was also the more banal matter of a monument for Mynster, for which contributions were being made. Here, too, Kierkegaard had no wish to be seen to interfere. But once Martensen was installed, and when against Kierkegaard's own inclinations a national liberal government was formed in the following December, the article immediately appeared. Among similar remarks, it said:

> A witness to the truth is a man whose life from first to last is unacquainted with everything called enjoyment. ... A witness to the truth, one of the authentic witnesses ... is a man who is scourged, maltreated, dragged from one prison to another ... and then at last ... crucified, or beheaded, or burned, or broiled on a grill, his lifeless body thrown away by the assistant executioner into a remote place, unburied — this is how a witness to the truth is buried![61]

In other words, it had been in circumstances quite unlike a fine ceremony where a high-ranking cleric in robes appoints a widely loved and respected predecessor to the holy ranks of those great witnesses who throughout history have suffered for their faith.

There was also the dating of the attack on the church itself. It began with fairly light artillery in a series of newspaper articles lasting from January to May. There, among other instructions, Kierkegaard told Mynster's newly appointed replacement to put an end to the 'official untruth' that what the priests were preaching was the New Testament.[62] As for Christianity, in Denmark there simply wasn't any.[63] Heavier calibre weaponry was kept in reserve until May.

This may well have been out of consideration for Regine. Although now married, in Copenhagen's collective short-term memory her name was still

---

61   *The Moment and Late Writings. Kierkegaard's Writings* XXIII, ed. and trans. Howard V. Hong and Edna H. Hong, Princeton, 1998, pp. 5-6.
62   Op. cit., p. 33, *Fædrelandet*, 22 March 1855.
63   Op. cit., pp. 35 and 39, *Fædrelandet*, January 1855.

inseparably linked with his. But on the 17th of March, 1855, Regine and Fritz Schlegel left for the West Indies where Schlegel had been appointed Governor of the Danish island colonies. The opening salvoes of a heavier barrage came with a frontal attack in the first issue of a self-financed broadsheet, the *Moment* (or *Instant* or more literally *The Twinkling of an Eye* [*Øieblikket*]). It appeared in May. The couple were by that time settling into their new life far from the scene of conflict.[64] The journal, or pamphlet, ran through nine issues, the tenth left incomplete. Readers reeled on finding descriptions of the clergy as 'liars', 'monkeys' and even 'cannibals'[65] and their church reduced to a 'pile of rubbish' that should be allowed to 'tumble down' so that, instead of 'making a fool of him in splendid edifices', people once more worshipped God 'in simplicity'.[66] Kierkegaard was obviously relishing his lone warrior role:

> *Was this what Christianity wanted: earnest in life and away with the honour and glory of vanity? — It all turned out the same, the change being this, that it took on the adjective 'Christian': the baubles of the orders, titles, rank etc. became Christian — and the priest (this of all ambiguities the most indecent ambiguity, this of all comicalities the most comical mish-mash [ruskumsnusk]), he is overjoyed to be, yes, decorated with 'the cross'. The cross! Yes, in Christendom's Christianity*

---

64 See Joakim Garff, *Kierkegaard's Muse: The Mystery of Regine Olsen*, trans. Alastair Hannay, Princeton, 2017, pp. 34-37.
65 *SKS* 13, *Øieblikket* 9, 24 Sept. 1855, pp. 376, 383/ *The Moment and Later Writings*, pp. 157-8*.
66 *SKS* 13, *Øieblikket* 4, 7 July 1855, p. 206/ *The Moment and Later Writings*, pp. 157-8*.

> the cross has become something like the child's hobbyhorse and trumpet.[67]

Some thought Kierkegaard had lost his mind. But he had his own explanation. It is to found on the first issue's opening page:

> Being an author — well yes, it gratifies me; to be honest I must say that I have been smitten in this producing — but please note in the way I wanted it. And what I've been in love with [up to now] is the opposite of having an instant effect, what I have loved is exactly remoteness from the moment: that distance in which, as one in love, I can follow at the heels of the thoughts, and as a pianist in love with his instrument entertain myself with language, coax forth expressions just as the thought requires — blissful pastime; not through an eternity could I become weary of this occupation! ... To fight with people — well, yes, it pleases me in a sense; I am so polemical by nature as to feel really in my element only when surrounded by mediocrity and meanness. But on one condition: that it is granted to me to despise in silence, to feed that passion that is in my soul, contempt, something for which my life as an author has given me ample opportunity.[68]

There follows a farewell to his reader, for he has now done with that blissful remoteness. Kierkegaard is about

---

67   SKS 13, *Øieblikket* 5, 27 July 1855, p. 236/ *The Moment and Later Writings*, pp. 157-8*.
68   SKS 13, *Øieblikket*, 1, p. 129/*The Moment and Later Writings*, pp. 157-158*.

to secure 'an instant effect' by going straight to the point in the here and now. Some readers may have guessed that in feeling that the end was near he was simply throwing caution to the winds and saying what had long been on his mind. We can guess that there may well be some truth in that.

The remains of an inherited fortune went to covering the journal's expenses and, with the tenth issue still incomplete, its editor and only contributor collapsed in the street on 2 October 1855. He was taken home but then at his own request admitted to hospital. He died there six weeks later, on 11 November, it is presumed of tuberculosis. Søren Aabye Kierkegaard was forty-two years old.

Behind the catchphrases

Most of those who nod knowingly on hearing the name can mention a few of the unusual titles and even identify some of their contents with as few catchphrases: 'Ah, yes, the leap of faith', 'Father of Existentialism', while those former majoring or even minoring philosophy students with a course on existentialism may well recall those 'three stages'.

All these and other tags are to a degree misleading. The 'leap of faith' captures a significant idea in some central works, but the expression is not one you will find anywhere in Kierkegaard's writing.[69] As for paternity, the words 'existential' and 'existentially' occur often enough, but they were not Kierkegaard's invention and his relationship to those many writers now tucked away under the existentialist label is, to say the least, ambiguous. As for the 'three stages', those on closer inspection don't appear at all like the graded ascent to religion proper promised, where reaching the top rung calls for a 'going for broke' leap into the absurd.

(a) The 'Leap'

If we look at the contexts in which the word 'leap' (*spring*) occurs, we find it in the expected connection

---

[69] As documented by Alastair McKinnon, 'Kierkegaard and "The Leap of Faith"', *Kierkegaardiana* 16, Copenhagen, pp. 107-122. McKinnon (p. 107) says: 'given all we now know about [Kierkegaard's] use of these [two] words ... it is almost unthinkable that he should have [used this phrase, i.e. the two in combination]'.

with faith in the two early pseudonymous works, *Fear and Trembling* and *Philosophical Crumbs*. The former is by that writer who looks on in wonder at Abraham's 'humble courage'[70] as the late-come father climbs a mountain with his son, intending to sacrifice him as proof of his faith. Beginning to reflect on the enormity of the situation, we may recollect that in scripture the long-awaited Isaac is also the promise of all future generations on earth. And in spite of the content of the divine command, it seems nevertheless crucial to the story's message, as told, that it is to his belief in '*this* life'[71] that Abraham holds on so firmly in what is, after all, in *Fear and Trembling* a clipped version of the journey to the mountain in Moriah. In the Bible it ends with a ram being providentially available for the slaughter, its horns caught in a bush.[72]

An everyday parallel is offered in the sharply contrasting shape of an imaginary tax collector, in whose behaviour there is not the slightest sign of the fact that he is resigned to the world having nothing to offer him in his need. His unfailing belief is that round every next corner things are nevertheless going to turn out well.[73]

> *Carefree as a devil-may-care good-for-nothing, he hasn't a worry in the world, and yet he purchases every moment that he lives, 'redeeming the seasonable time' at the dearest price.*[74]

There is talk here of a 'movement of infinity' that may easily sound like that unwritten 'leap of faith'. It is said that 'the movement of faith must be made continually

---

70   SKS 4, p. 143 *Fear and Trembling*, p. 77.
71   SKS 4, p. 117/ *Fear and Trembling*, p. 53.
72   Gen. 23.14.
73   SKS 4, pp. 133 ff./ *Fear and Trembling*, pp. 68 ff.
74   SKS 4, p. 135 / *Fear and Trembling*, p. 69.

on the strength of the absurd'.⁷⁵ But what does that mean? It sounds as though there were, at a further level of unintelligibility, the need for a continual leaping that, with the teacher constantly in mind, sustains acceptance of the absurd over a stretch of time. Or could it be a matter of a sustained momentum, in which the notion of a leap is hard to place but somehow sets things going? But then we have to bear in mind that faith does not place something in our hands, something that we can then keep hold of, as though it were from then on in our possession.

Of actual leaps, we can read of an unsuccessful attempt by the author. With the 'one, two, three' of a 'trampoline leap', he can go 'upside down in existence' and into 'infinitude', but what he cannot do is come down again on his feet. But that was precisely what Abraham did all the way to the mountain, as though nothing had happened.⁷⁶

Is this because Johannes *de silentio* is talking, as the name indicates, of things that *he* cannot understand or communicate, either to a reader or to himself, and so understandably holds his tongue about, or says, as here, that it is beyond him? If so, are we ourselves assumed to be confined with him in this communicational dead zone? Or is it that we are meant to see the point of a superior particularity, one in which we rise (by leaping?) to a level above Johannes *de silentio*, a level on which, if only Isaac could join us, we would be able to explain to him what Abraham had in mind, and in words that his son would understand?

Another description distinguishes between 'knights of infinity' and 'knights of faith'. The former 'jump' to infinitude and come back to earth, but on landing they

---

75   SKS 4, p. 132/*Fear and Trembling*, p. 67.
76   SKS 4, p. 131/*Fear and Trembling*, p. 66.

are unable to hide a 'vacillation', in which their leap upwards has made them strangers to the finitude they return to. Perhaps we would find ourselves faltering similarly when trying to explain things to Isaac. In other words, these knights of infinity are no longer steadfast believers in *this* life, while, as the text nicely puts it, the knight of faith hits the ground walking: in 'transform[ing] the leap in life to a gait' he 'expresses the sublime in the pedestrian absolutely'.[77]

Philosophical Crumbs takes up the theme of absurdity (and paradox) aired only briefly in *Fear and Trembling*. It does so in the cooler atmosphere of a philosophical speculation about the conditions under which a historical event, an event in time, can have a bearing on our 'eternal happiness'. It is something Christianity assumes, but that particular religion is not mentioned and the discussion is abstract enough to meet any Hegelian opposition on equal terms. There are a handful of references to a leap, but the crucial one concerns the way in which people have taken God's existence to be something that can or must be proved. In this context, we may think of the leap as what you need to make once you find that the alleged steps in the proof fail to reach the conclusion.

But the author then points out that the stance you adopt when aiming to *prove* God's existence is one where you are *suspending* belief. This implies that in some way or guise the belief must already have been there. You may begin to doubt, but if you try to recapture the belief, the means you adopt to replace it will leave you worrying less about God's existence than about how to patch up the proof. However, it was doubt that put you in mind of the need for proof in the

---

[77] SKS 4, p. 135/*Fear and Trembling*, p. 70.

first place, while what you need is the kind of certainty, or certitude, with which you began, before doubt was put in its path, whether this faith is an inherited belief or due to a choice of your own. One of many positive references to Socrates characterizes that tireless Greek debater as someone who 'constantly assumed God existed', and who did all he could to 'permeate existence with the idea of purpose'.[78] The leap mentioned here in *Philosophical Crumbs* is one that you take if you find yourself wasting time in the fruitless academic exercise of trying to prove God's existence. You do so by letting go of the proof and allowing 'existence' to return. This is *your* 'contribution', just a 'little moment' but one that also to be 'taken into account'. The same author will say two years later in *Postscript* that it is 'an evasion to escape the strenuousness of action and risk' and to 'bring the problem to bear on the realm of knowledge and chat'. He will also say that '[i]f I am truly to venture, and truly strive for the highest good, there must be uncertainty, and I must, if I may put it in this way, have room to move'.

> *But the largest space I can move in, where there is room enough for the most intense gesture of the passion of the infinite, is uncertainty of knowledge regarding an eternal happiness, or the fact that the choice is in a finite sense madness.*[79]

We note, then, that here it is not the choice that is the leap but this contribution of ours that returns us to the 'largest space'.

The lesson of *Philosophical Crumbs* is, to repeat, that all we have to go on is the 'teacher' in time. As a paradox,

---

78   S*KS* 4, pp. 247-249/*Philosophical Crumbs*, pp. 115-116.
79   *SKS* 7, 3, pp.87-388/*CUP*, pp. 357-358.

the Incarnation is in rational terms an absurdity. But it is one that those who wish to draw wisdom from it must accept. It is also why whatever you believe in faith is not 'knowledge',[80] not something about the eternal that you can retain like a piece of 'real estate'.[81] What we choose to receive from the teacher is a 'condition' that we take on trust. With error inherent in our existence, it is not even something we can accuse God of having taken *from* us (as if he, and not we by 'virtue' of confinement to existence, had planted the snake in the Garden of Eden). We are not to believe a *doctrine* that lets us assume we have 'got it' and which elevates us out of time. All our business with eternity is bound up with the teacher,[82] one who is a historical figure that we accept in a moment out of (our) time as the eternal *in* time.

'Given' the condition, not as a gift but as a working assumption of our own, we can then be shown what needs to be done: learning from the example we gain a sense of the ways in which we are 'in error'[83] and may approach the perfection we can never reach.

In his next publication two years later, as noted earlier, and surprisingly for Anglophone readers, Johannes Climacus says that God does not exist. Again, this is not to say that there is no God, but that God is nowhere to be found within the space-time limits of the world in which *we* exist. In the Latin sense of 'exist' (*exsistere*, to emerge, arise, or stand out from), God 'is' or 'has being', but being eternal there is nothing he can emerge from. God does not 'think' but 'creates',[84] which at this stage of

---

80 *SKS* 4, p. 263/*Philosophical Crumbs*, p. 131.
81 *SKS* 4, p. 295/*Philosophical Crumbs*, p. 162.
82 *SKS* 4, p. 223/*Philosophical Crumbs*, p. 93. For purposes of abstraction, the text has 'the god'.
83 *SKS* 4, pp. 255, 295/*Philosophical Crumbs*, pp. 122, 162.
84 *SKS* 7, p. 303/*CUP*, p. 278.

the creative proceedings he does through us, or which in less anthropomorphic terms, *is* done through us.

As we know, Johannes in *Postscript* ridicules the idea that subjective thinkers might form a club. Lessing would understand that. We find the ever-useful Lessing declining an invitation from the philosopher Jacobi to join him in a '*salto mortale*' into the eternal, a 'beyond' that history (time) can never reach, or which, if that is where you imagine you now find yourself, never reaches history. Lessing admonishes Jacobi for supposing that by holding hands they could leap together, each giving the other support: 'When you are to leap you must do it alone, also be alone in properly understanding that it is an impossibility'. There follows the irony for which Lessing was famous: his head is 'too heavy' and his legs 'too old' for him to do it alone.[85]

As an Enlightenment figure, Lessing would in any case regard a leap beyond the range of human powers of illumination as unnecessary. But he might still, in the role of subjective thinker in which he is appealed at the beginning of the larger second part of *Postscript*, have some sympathy for the idea of a divinity as remote or as un-existential as in Johannes Climacus's conception. With a deity beyond our powers of comprehension, and so totally unlike us, for one with even the lightest of heads and the most athletic legs a leap that far would be virtual suicide, not least as far as returning to earth is concerned. The irony here may be subtler than we assumed.

The leap also makes an appearance in *The Concept of Anxiety*. It is there to distinguish Christianity from both Greek and Judaic religiousness. The point here is purely conceptual, a matter of words. The two latter religions assume that we live in a perfectible world where a

---

85   *SKS* 7, pp. 99-100/*CUP*, pp. 86-87.

'quantitative' accumulation can in principle one day remove all imperfection, while an essential part of the Christian narrative is the 'Fall'. If, as a professed Christian, we hear that the source of life-truths must be taken on trust in an example whose own being (a combination of time and eternity) defies understanding, that too is something that we may just nod to while continuing as before.

What, then, we may also ask, can be said of the leap in Kierkegaard's own case? Did he make such a leap or several? Or should we say that his life was one long leap from the beginning? Was it the faith of the tax collector or an Abraham, a seemingly irrational and anxiety allaying trust that something will turn up round every next corner? But what if that was true? Wouldn't such ignoring of all actual and practical considerations, obstacles to desired outcomes that he well knew were in the way, be tantamount to madness? Might it not be better said, more calmly, that just as his pseudonym has said of Socrates, that Kierkegaard 'constantly assumed God existed' and that he did so even when things did not go well for him personally or went very badly?[86]

We read in the journals of how Kierkegaard's relation to Christianity could suffer. In said that in his youth he found the version he inherited at home 'emasculating'.[87] Later the Christianity outside the home, the 'Christendom' that he derided, he found to be mere show or theatre. Yet, in spite of a period of Faustian rebellion while he was still home-bound, and whatever depths he may have reached in periods of melancholia, Kierkegaard seems never actually to have abandoned his faith; or to put it otherwise, his faith seems never to have abandoned him. However derogatory his views

---

86 *SKS* 18, JJ:115, p. 177 / *KJN* 2, p. 164.
87 *SKS* 14, AA:15, p. 32 / *KJN* 1, p. 28.

on Denmark's Christendom, his personal attitude to Christianity seems not unlike a piece of inherited 'real estate' but owned in the form of strictly private property. That he should start looking for a proof (and in doing so lose the deeds of ownership) seems out of the question, as much as there might be any occasion or period where Kierkegaard found himself needing a leap to renew association with the 'eternal'.

Yet it might be so. His work contains literary expressions that suggest a familiarity with melancholia may well have got the better of an inborn or inherited trust in life. It would, of course, be hard to imagine a subjective thinker not having in mind the absurdity on which faith depends; it may even have been a permanent lodger in the basement of his busy mind or, when coming up to street-level, a supplement to its quotient of 'pathos'. But in a life filled with existential hazards, who other than those escapists who call on their intellects to give them a license to believe really care about the paradox? And who else would do that but those who turn religion into an academic discipline and seek a redemption that is just a matter of putting words in the right order and acquiescing in what they say, if they haven't already done so before they started? Those with a living sense of the options, the sufferers, will not let intellect stand in the way of redemption. Writing of what he is made to admit is something that lies beyond his powers of comprehension, Johannes *de silentio* is no simpleton and he presents the choice with some skill and an insight that readers may feel stem from the real author in something more than a literary exercise:

> *If there no eternal consciousness in a man, if at the bottom of everything there were*

> *only a wild ferment, a power that twisting in dark passions produced everything great or inconsequential; if an unfathomable, insatiable emptiness lay hid beneath everything, what would life be but despair. If it were thus, if there were no sacred bond uniting mankind, if one generation rose up after another like the leaves of the forest, if one generation succeeded another as the songs of birds in the woods, if the human race passed through the world as a ship through the sea or the wind through the desert, a thoughtless and fruitless whim, if an eternal oblivion always lurked hungrily for its prey and there were no power strong enough to wrest it from its clutches, how empty and devoid of comfort would life be!*

Johannes's conclusion is: 'for that reason it is not so.'[88] But the language, however literary, is that of someone imagined or real who has faced the possibility that it might be so.

Could this persisting possibility be at the heart of Kierkegaard's melancholia? This is someone who could say 'how terrible is my doubt'.[89] But then again, the 'it is not so' could equally be the reassurance of someone reverting to an inalienable belief of the kind that Kierkegaard had met with as a child in his father's unaffected faith. It is, for these believers even if liable to pangs of doubt, an essential feature in the structure of human being, an 'existential' in Heidegger's sense, though that 'down-to-the-basics' philosopher would not

---

88 *SKS* 4, p. 112 / *Fear and Trembling*, p. 49.
89 *SKS* 19, Not. 7:17, p. 210/*KJN* 3, p. 206.

include it in his own list. Less than some specific truth, it is closer to an inextinguishable even if at times fragile faith in existence itself. In the most general expression that Kierkegaard's undoubting pseudonyms provide, and whatever doubts lurked in his melancholia, it is faith in the self being 'grounded' in 'something else'.

This doesn't mean in other selves, as both post-Hegelian and existentialist philosophers have urged, or in forces of nature: it means having a ground in whatever these also have their origin and meaning. In the words of his super-Christian pseudonym, refusing to accept this would come under the most glaring form of despair among those whose faces *The Sickness unto Death* would later bring to light.

Related to the above is Kierkegaard's comment in one place that the best proof of the 'soul's immortality, God's existence (etc.)' is that his father told him so.[90] That connects with another comment about managing up until now to press things 'only to the point of being a perfectly simple Christian'.[91] With but little further ado we have someone who, as one writer puts it, was 'without rival in the art of attacking reason with its own weapons',[92] engaging in an attack-is-the-best-defence campaign on behalf of his father's stubborn faith and, in doing so, deploying the same intellectual arsenal as that with which the new liberals were making their facile appropriation of Christianity.

One who liked a fight and felt 'really in [his] element' when surrounded by 'mediocrity and meanness', would feel even more at home facing down an intellectual elite that had turned the living word into learned talk. An underlying sub-textual thread may be traced here.

---

90   *SKS* 20, NB5:114, p. 417/*KJN* 4, p. 418*.
91   *SKS* 22, NB11:204, p. 127/*KJN* 6, p. 125*.
92   William Heinesen, *The Doomed Fiddlers*, p. 144, my translation.

It begins on a desolate heath, where God had been cursed long before Kierkegaard's birth, and extends to Kierkegaard himself at forty-one writing in the year before he died of God's absence. He interprets it as the divine punishment of being ignored and left to his own devices.[93]

(b) 'Existentialist'

A simple tale, all too simple but nevertheless useful and not far from the mark, can explain the rise of Existentialism. It goes as follows. With the breakdown of theologically backed and classical ideals of authority, a crisis arose in philosophy, first in the Renaissance and then in the period known as the Enlightenment. The 'knee-jerk' reaction was to rescue authority as such. This was done, first subjectively in the realm of ideas (idealism), as befitted the renewed humanism of the Renaissance, and later, objectively, in the search for natural laws through observation (positivism). Neither route to certainty or intelligibility left room for the thinker or observer as 'existing' human beings. These were supposedly taken care of in what the mind could find in itself or in whatever order of things nature could reveal to an open-minded observation undistorted by passing or inbred personal perspectives. The details of a person's life might well be of interest to novelists, but they had no theoretical part to play in the larger scheme, any more than they will in the long-awaited 'theory of everything'. If and when delivered, it too will be a theory of no one.

In brief, what were once thought to be the prerogatives of theology and classical humanism, were channelled in Existentialism wholesale to the empty-handed

---

[93] *SKS* 26, NB34:34, pp. 344-345/*KJN* 10, p. 353.

individual. 'Authentic' individuals were those that took personal responsibility for what they became. Readers of *Either/Or* will detect some pre-echo of that in Wilhelm's talk of 'choosing' oneself 'absolutely'.[94] The self to be chosen is the one we find ourselves *as* we are on waking up to *what* we are. Birth deals a hand of cards and while the face values of some remain the same to our dying day, others take time to show their value. There are leanings, temperament, abilities, gender and sexuality, and on top of that, or underneath, a variably rigid or malleable social role. So, while plain geographical and ethnic properties recorded in our birth certificates and identity cards may stay the same, others have their destiny in the future. How it turns out can be our own doing, less or more, but in *Either /Or* Wilhelm insists on the latter: the 'self-aware' individual is conscious of being 'this definite individual', equipped with 'these aptitudes, these tendencies, these instincts, these passions, influenced by these definite surroundings, as this definite product of a definite outside world'. And this individual 'assumes responsibility for it all',[95] not of course for the way in which it arrives on the worldly scene, but for what it becomes thereafter.

What, then, is this 'all'? For Wilhelm, it is the functioning of a society to which his own role as a minor court judge and his marriage both contribute, the one to its maintenance and the other to its ordered continuation. There is little hint of Existentialism's focus on the individual in that description, and as it stands it might well qualify as an outline of the ideals of a socialist society. But in recommending his young friend,

---

94   *SKS* 3, p. 213/*Either/Or*, p. 523.
95   *SKS* 3, p. 239/*Either/Or*, p. 542.

the protagonist of *Either/Or*'s first part, to choose a socially responsible version of selfhood like his , in preference to a 'non'-self that merely exploits whatever the world offers in the way of aesthetic satisfaction, is a step in the existentialist direction. On the other hand, habit and social convention, which were presumably the burden and result of Wilhelm's own choice, are exactly what Existentialism's critics would complained that its real exponents failed to address. They speak, instead, of the social benefits of consensus and the commonplace, of corporation and regulated association, and of a self-improving community under freely associating 'we' identities that include democratically elected political parties, these allowing open discussion and majority-rule by general agreement. The largely socialist and Marxist critics of Existentialism saw 'decadence' and 'moral narcissism' in the existentialist ideal of self-seeking authenticity[96] and would leave soul-searching to artists and others to play and 'create' out of harm's way on society's perimeter. More crucially, they accused Existentialism of failing to take account of history and the changing contexts that limit the range and content of the choices they so much applauded.

Existentialists claimed in return to be undermining deep-rooted habits that shielded people from opportunities of *social* creativity, where these are often to be found especially in the outer fringes of a society and at its dissident edges. They pointed to the harmful effect of herd thinking and the socially as well as individually anaesthetizing effect of habit and convention.

This sounds closer to Kierkegaard. That he deserves

---

96   See Norberto Bobbio, *The Philosophy of Decadentism: A Study in Existentialism*, Oxford: Blackwell, 1948, and Georgi Lukács, *Existentialisme ou marxisme?*, Paris: Nagel, 1948.

the 'father' title as a precursor will seem too obvious to need discussion. Few self-styled existentialist authors, even or especially those given the label but inclined to disown it, could fail to recognize his influence or acknowledge their debt. Even if Kierkegaard himself might pour scorn on members of a widespread *cult* of so-called single selves collectively 'going it alone', his influence is to be seen, felt or read in many such circles.

Some famous writers caught on quite early. Henrik Ibsen secured a copy of *Either/Or* and read it in Danish, which at that time was almost identical to his own Norwegian. German translation followed, then French and English, making Kierkegaard available to an ever wider and more varied readership. In Spain, Miguel de Unamuno, born nine years after Kierkegaard's death, traced his own thought back to both Pascal and Kierkegaard, the latter evident with regard to the two themes of sorrow and evil, the one without resolution and the other with no place for redemption: to recognize this was to be aware of the brotherhood of man. Unamuno's Russian contemporary, Lev Shestov, found his way to existentialism through Shakespeare's *Hamlet* ('The time is out of joint')[97] but on reading Kierkegaard later in life found the latter's writing much to his taste. Writers as diverse as Dostoevsky, Kafka, Genet, Samuel Becket, and John Updike, and the film-makers Ingmar Bergmann and Jean Luc-Godard, are part of the spiritual diaspora whose centre had been a loner writing in a series of apartments within a walled city in a small European state, and whose writing 'machine' was fuelled by a literary imagination that drew from his own experience.

As for philosophers or 'thinkers', the very fact that 'Existentialism' was on so many people's lips presented them with an Either/Or of their own. Some, for

---

97   End of Act 1, sc. V.

personal or ideological reasons, welcomed the role of philosophical spokesman for a widespread movement for which they could assume the role of guru, or else felt a social responsibility for explicating the thought that lay unarticulated in widespread manifestations of its 'idea'. Others shunned such association, preferring to keep their well-grounded existentialist thoughts for those who could understand the reasons for them.

Among the disowners was the seminal 'existentialist' thinker Martin Heidegger, who nevertheless acknowledged his considerable borrowing from Kierkegaard. With a theological background and enough religion in his thought to seek a Christian burial, Heidegger came to decline the existentialist label, as did Gabriel Marcel more emphatically. With his clear religious agenda, Marcel had no wish to be associated with the professed atheist Jean-Paul Sartre, whose wide following had given Existentialism a populist atheistic label and identity that it lacked when first introduced to France.[98] He, Sartre, on the other hand, was so impressed by the sheer impact of Kierkegaard's writing as to want to have him aboard in spite of their differences. He came to bestow on Kierkegaard the historical honour of having shown 'perhaps for the first time' that 'the universal enters into history as the singular'. A place for Kierkegaard was also reserved with the still living as an 'adventurer', a category to which as instances of the 'singular universal' we all potentially belong.[99]

Like Sartre, also a novelist and dramatist, other recognized philosophers welcomed a wider existentialist

---

98 Singularly by Jean Wahl in his *Études Kierkegaardiennes*, Paris: Aubier,1938: Vrin 1967, which presented Kierkegaard to France as a philosopher and not just a theologian and one to be reckoned with.

99 Jean-Paul Sartre, 'The Singular Universal', in Josiah Thompson (ed.), *Kierkegaard: A Collection of Critical Essays*, New York, 1972, p. 257.

response to their work. Among them was the German philosopher Karl Jaspers. Coming to philosophy through medicine and psychiatry, he came to believe in the ability of existentialist philosophy to replace science as a panacea for the ills of our tragic and 'out of joint' times.

And yet, were a tag or easy label to be found for the encyclopaedist, it would be one that identified the core of Existentialism as it developed in the twentieth century in its own article of faith: that the centre and generator of all value is individual freedom. This, in particular, is the side of Existentialism that invites the criticism that it ignores history and the way in which both values and opportunities are determined by circumstances that change with time. For human freedom, surely, is not only constrained by those circumstances, it is also defined by them.

It is less easy to include Kierkegaard, however, among those most obviously exposed to that objection. Even Sartre honoured him for introducing subjective choice *into* history and a comment by Kierkegaard himself shows that he was not unaware of the relation of his own thought to historical change. He claimed that his category of the single individual was where history was heading: 'the evolution of the whole world tends toward the absolute significance singularity's category.' And this was 'precisely the principle of Christianity'.[100]

Industrialization and the growth of urbanism would prove him right as far as the atomizing of traditionally collective elements in society was concerned, with a corresponding depersonalizing due to loss of those protective *collective* identities. These very developments were tailor-made for the anxieties that Kierkegaard's own personal situation invited in a country that aside from its overseas trade was still largely agricultural. Then as now the 'natural' response to the fragility of

---

100   *SKS* 20, NB:123, p. 88 /*KJN* 4, p. 87.

singularity was nevertheless to focus on those collective identities formed in a fight for respect and equal rights under banners of 'equality'. We have in our own time a proliferation of 'we'-consolidating labels defining selves that adopt politically topical identities in terms of ethnic, economic, and gender differentia. It is not clear what bright future is envisaged in this focus on collective identity, one that includes collective differences or one that turns a blind eye to the differentia and focuses on rights, manners, and stabilizes society through established rules of equity. If, one fine day, we are able to ignore any un-remediable remainders of colour, gender, cultural background, custom and heritage, we will be paying each other mutual respect at a properly universal level. Implicit here is an abstract ideal of equity that puts all heritages or what remains of them on an equal plane. That harmonizes with well-entrenched Enlightenment ideals. Seen otherwise, it could spell an artificial cultural uniformity that means the ultimate in colonization: a mannered society that feigns respect and conceals disdain for what, individually, people really are.

And what are they? Kierkegaard's pseudonyms insist that we are in each case the 'concrete' self, with its 'aptitudes, predispositions, etc.',[101] where these have been acquired 'in this set of circumstances'. It is this or that 'definite product of a definite outside world'[102] that should be the focus of moral concern, a concern which, we may assume, is itself developed through a cultivation of spirit. We may also assume that among the 'fruits' of such cultivation is an ability to appreciate the place within cultural diversity to which spirit in each case owes its own origins.

---

101 SKS 11, p. 182, cf. p. 171/*The Sickness unto Death*, p. 99, cf. p. 86.
102 SKS 3, p. 239/*Either/Or*, p. 542.

That Kierkegaard would resist the 'Existentialist' label seems beyond doubt. The very 'ist'-ending shouts 'universal' in the bad sense, just as to make the point clearer — and should the term ever come to be coined — would an 'Exceptionalist' label. As he notes in an open-hearted journal entry from 1849, the year of *The Sickness unto Death*, as well as three signed works:

> *The particular is the exception and should be conscious of being so; indeed, instead of counseling others to do the same, the exception should counsel them to follow the universal.*

Shown a compendium list of those bearing the Existentialist tag, a Kierkegaard now at rest and above the fray would surely see the point of his inclusion, perhaps even be proud of it. He had brought matters that concern each of us into the forum of truth finding. But as someone who claimed in that same entry that 'the particular is only true when it has the character of primitivity, in relation to God',[103] and who saw himself as at God's disposal, he would not want to be identified with those of whom it is said that individual freedom is the centre and generator of all value.

(c) The Three-Stage Ladder

In broad outline, the itinerary that Johannes Climacus provides for the subjective thinker is aimed at that subject-to-subject meeting with God. Without a self to start with it would never occur, so any expectation of such a meeting requires overcoming the environment's hold on the way in which you make your life meaningful. Otherwise there is nothing on which the through-time stability for anything worth calling selfhood is able to

---

103   *SKS* 22, NB 11:183, 110/*KJN* 6, p. 107.

gain a foothold. You acquire this stability by choosing to make your 'self'-constituting' set of attributes and capacities recognizable within that complex of interdependent identity-roles that we call 'society'.

But the subject-to-subject relationship also requires *in*dependence, and that means (apart from the paradox of the particular being prior to the universal) that you must blur or lower your gaze on social aspiration and on recognition and the psychological reinforcement of whatever personal pride it affords, and raising your sights to focus on a common source of human value beyond all divisions. It is to be held on to firmly, even grimly, and in the face of pressures to bow to one or another 'idol' that does secular service for the 'eternal'. The strength with which you do so is where 'truth' for the human being is found.

These moves correspond to those three main stages, aesthetic, ethical and religious, for which Kierkegaard is so widely known. In religious terms the aesthetic stage is a non-starter. The only self here is a set of aptitudes tapping into sources of accessible gratification and thus at the mercy of what the world has or can be made to offer in this respect. Attempting to take control of the sources merely deadens the capacity to be gratified and leads to endless repetition and a lowering of the level of satisfaction, which then leads to a search for further opportunities. The ethical stage 'reveals' a diachronic self for all to see in its civic role and status, but it does so at a level at which the particular is still subordinate to the universal. In other words, it is, as yet, just a platform for launching the further move to a one-to-one relationship to God. As *Fear and Trembling* points out, when 'the ethical is the universal and as such, in turn, the divine', it reaches the divine only through social duties being 'referred' to God. It is like being a soldier whose relation to the general is not one the general knows anything about: there is no 'enter[ing] into relation with God in the duty itself'.[104]

My hopes for myself must therefore be found in something beyond personal ambition, something that puts any thoughts in that direction in the shade although not out of sight. That 'something' takes the form, first, of a passionate yet object-less longing, a yearning in which, to take myself, I suppress my 'relative' goals in time in favour of one that is 'absolute' but with as yet no clear idea of how these goals figure in this relation of subordination to the absolute. In particular, I have no idea of the absolute having to be accessible in this life at some point in time as the goal of *Postscript*'s itinerary presupposes. So far, it is an abstract Archimedean point, and as dimensionless and space-saving as geometrical points officially are. Being nowhere, it may just as well be anywhere or everywhere. This is 'Religiousness A', and according to Johannes it can exist even in 'paganism',[105] where divinity is all around us and is just for that reason not available for one-to-one relationships.

For the ultimate relationship to be made, the subject must 'become aware of how the dialectical ... knocks him down into the pathos of the absurd'.[106] The absolute is nowhere to be seen, and is quite beyond our ken, but can be focused on by the single self in a passionate inwardness that owes nothing to external authority. This is 'Religiousness B' and identified by Johannes Climacus as Christianity, with the 'teacher in time' . With it come those notions and senses of guilt and sin.

---

104 *SKS* 4, p. 60/*Fear and Trembling*, p. 96.
105 *SKS* 7, p. 506/*CUP*, p. 466.
106 *SKS* 7, pp. 505-506/*CUP*, pp. 465-466.

This 'dialectic' (of eternal/finite) naturally doesn't conjure forth God the eternal 'subject'. For that to happen there has to be belief in the possibility of the eternal God *becoming* 'subject'. In an easily overlooked footnote Johannes adds a comment to his provocative claim that truth lies in *how* you believe and not in *what* you believe. He says that God is a 'postulate', a necessary assumption but with its necessity coming from the thinker — an 'existing' thinker who *has* to postulate God, the alternative being despair. Necessity here has the existential sense of 'need'.[107]

The 'ladder' implicit in Johannes's surname is one on which he climbs to the next highest rung. His own virtue for the reader is in *not* having reached the top. There he would simply disappear from view and his humour, if verbalized, would be of the 'absolutely isolated' kind that 'subsists in the person alone'. From a mundane point of view, the Christianity the knight of faith practises is plainly absurd, and the knight of faith, as we know, can still be mundane. If visible or audible, among bystanders, his or her humour would invite laughter of a 'just look at that!' kind. We are given an example of the isolated humour of one with faith: it would be the 'infinite comedy' of saying 'Thou to God' in 'the infinite pathos of religiousness' and then turning around and repeating this personal form of address aloud to the deity while in the company of others, some of whom can also be addressed in the second person singular. As in all comedy, there is contradiction; here it is that of the vocative form of address having a quite different force in each case. There would be the humour of bathos in talking to God as you would to your neighbour. A subjective thinker who reaches that top rung has thus to be 'bifrontal',[108] that is to say, able to look both ways

---

107 *SKS* 7, p. 183/*CUP*, pp. 169 fn.
108 *SKS* 7, pp. 88-89 /*CUP*, p. 76.

and know the difference between speaking in isolation *to* God and speaking in company *about* God.

But this side, too, must have its proper subject. Johannes marks off two boundaries, one between the aesthetic and ethical stages and the other between ethical and religious. They have their respective modes: irony for the one and humour for the other. The self that is able to establish the relationship to God has made the transition by coming inside the boundary zone that is humour. The ironist puts on a show of superiority over an environment that in the life-view of the aesthete has been too much in control. However, there is in this boundary area still no 'I' but just an ironical downstaging of the world in general from an indeterminate position still lacking an independent occupant.

Irony is nevertheless a beginning. It is that 'cultivation of spirit',[109] an unstable 'nowhere' between two life-views that leaves the individual suspended in a stressful balancing act between emphasizing the 'I' on the one hand, and on the other a culture that is impervious to individual selves and 'infinitely abstracts' from any personal 'I'.[110] *Either/Or* had claimed that the tension is resolved by culture welcoming aboard one more visibly social self, the 'I' then reaping the rewards of disclosure with the enrichments of personal identity made possible by diachronicity, all of it so conscientiously detailed by Wilhelm. In Wilhelm's eyes that seems to be enough in spite of his admission, almost as an afterthought, that a misfit whose life has no such protection from life's vicissitudes might find a way of relating to the universal precisely as an 'I'.

It is this afterthought that holds the three stages together as rungs on the ladder as the nature of the

---

109   *SKS* 7, p. 457/*CUP*, p. 422.
110   Ibid.

progression or ascent later emerges, not the substance of Wilhelm's extensive defence of marriage as a way of realizing the universal. In order to find Wilhelm a place on Johannes's ladder we must therefore focus narrowly on his last few pages and perhaps look for other explanations of his spirited defence of the ethical.

And those final pages themselves contain more of some importance for the way in which the progression is to be interpreted. A 'final word' is attached to Wilhelm's second letter: a sermon enclosed in correspondence from another friend, a priest in Jutland, that largely agricultural part of Denmark where the Kierkegaard family had its roots.

In Socratic terms, a sermon belonging to a stabilized Christian existence speaks *from* Christianity as it is preached. It is of little help in getting readers to make a new start, but taking readers back to the beginning to let them start afresh was, according to Kierkegaard's later and posthumously published appraisal of his own work, the very aim of the 'dialectical' works under the 'Johannes' pseudonyms. By presenting his young friend's views before responding to them, there is indeed some semblance of dialogue in Wilhelm's two letters. But he gives little evidence of being a subjective thinker, or even a Hegelian consciously participating in a dialectic whose future he sees himself playing a part in. He is able to tell his friend not to 'sneeze at' the sermon just because the priest who has yet to give it had written that he was sure he could make 'every farmer understand it'. In this way, Wilhelm is made to convey to the reader that the universal is accessible to everyone, not just to those, like all the priests in Denmark, with degrees in theology. Wilhelm's 'last word' is that 'the beauty of the universal consists precisely in *everyone* being able to understand it'.[111]

---

111   SKS 3, p. 318/*Either/Or*, p. 594.

However little aware he is of being a participant in Johannes's dialectical itinerary, in his real author's hands Wilhelm is nevertheless in these closing pages handing over a question for others to take over, as with a baton in a relay race. What question? The obvious answer, surely, is how an 'I' deprived of a social diachronicity so prized by Wilhelm can find another form of selfhood that presents exceptionality in another and 'nobler' light.

But there is also something closer to home in Wilhelm's defence of marriage. It has what speech-act theorists call a 'performative' function, an aim produced by the words being uttered but not contained in their literal meaning. In fact, there are two such, not for Wilhelm himself but for the real author: the defence of marriage contains two unwritten messages to Regine.

Of *Either/Or* Kierkegaard writes, 'I wrote it for *her*'. 'The Diary of a Seducer' was designed to 'repel' Regine, a strategy that the intelligent young lady would easily see through, and a wiser thought might have been that the 'Diary' would give her public support for escaping a match with such a scoundrel. By the time the then two-volume work was published neither strategy would count and, to Kierkegaard's surprise, he was not 'hated, reviled, etc.' but became 'a brilliant success'.[112]

But there is also a more deeply embedded message to be found in Wilhelm's contribution, although it would take time to decode it. Kierkegaard wrote in the year before his death that what he had written in Wilhelm's name was 'what one could expect from a married man who champions marriage with ethical enthusiasm'.[113] There is a distance implied in this, and the fact that the book's editor's name translates as 'triumphant hermit' suggests that the real author's sympathies, however

---

112   *SKS* 25, NB28:54, p. 257/*KJN* 5, pp. 259-260.
113   *SKS* 25, NB29:113, p. 375/*KJN* 9, p. 379.

contained, lay closer to the aesthete than to his puppet ethicist. By the time Kierkegaard had written *Stages*, this had in any case become a fact. In this work, where both *Either/Or*'s editor Victor Eremita and the notorious Seducer (also named 'Johannes') appear, the latter talks about women as 'bait'. Now, in the year before his death nine years later, Kierkegaard says there is 'much truth' in that, and he writes of 'lust for life' as the woman's prerogative, but also as what men project into their relationships with them. Refraining from doing so is to give their initial spiritual potential a better chance. The Seducer and his reclusive editor are now presented as one. The former has 'the whole 'Christian ascetic view of woman ... at his fingertips', and the only difference between him and the triumphant hermit who has risen above marriage is in the directions they take.[114]

The ethical stage as presented by Wilhelm simply drops out of view. Instead of a sequel developing the status of *Either/Or* as a rung or series of rungs on the ladder, *Stages on Life's Way* appears actually to invite a return to the problem to which the ethical stage was offered there prematurely. It failed to provide a foothold for religion at the B-level, and now it even stands in the way, so that preparation for that extra requires stepping down again to the area of irony, where spirit is cultivated in an '*I*'-'*We*' tension and perhaps even, prior to that, down to a development within the aesthetic, where, as *Fear and Trembling* puts it, the '*I*' can be involved in 'mood, feeling, etc.'. *Fear and Trembling* had already hinted at this by saying that wanting to 'stay inside, or slide back' into the 'inner determinant of mood, feeling etc.', is to '[commit] an offence ...'.[115] But that might be the precisely the Either/Or context out of which the nobler

---

114   *SKS* 25, NB29:113, pp. 375-376/*KJN* 9, pp. 379-380.
115   *SKS* 4, p. 161/*Fear and Trembling*, p. 97.

exception, by meeting these challenges, is able to form a new relationship to the universal.

Postscript doesn't go that far. But its author, who having been part of it is familiar with the preceding pseudonymous production, seems to speak for those whose journey to faith is less of a challenge than it is for the intended readers, namely Denmark's cultural élite. Johannes Climacus says that it would be quite wrong to 'bring down the dangers and terrors of intellectual warfare' on one whose 'modest contentment is his 'earthly bliss'. That seems to saying that the paradox can be left to philosophers and shouldn't worry those who want to follow the conventions, including marriage. There's nothing wrong in following custom. On the other hand, he is not surprised that many intellectuals 'well on the way with world history and the future of mankind', and who think that marriage presents no problem, react to being told that it is not that easy. He has read 'carefully' what has been written on marriage in both *Either/Or* and *Stages on Life's Way* and thinks that even though Wilhelm cannot be blamed for his 'eager enthusiasm', he is certain that 'if only he can get hold of him' and 'whisper a little secret in his ear', the judge will admit that 'difficulties remain'.[116]

Assuming that Johannes would still be there to catch the comment, a Kierkegaard in his final years might have whispered something in his old pseudonym's ear. Hasn't Johannes seen that the views of Wilhelm's young friend, expressed with such sympathy and with an eloquence equal to that of his own spirited defence of marriage, were those that he too, Kierkegaard himself has later shared? He might even have confessed to having entertained them at the time of writing that enthusiastic defence of marriage.

---

116 *SKS* 7, p. 167 *CUP*, p. 152.

Take an example. Among the disparaging comments on marriage that Wilhelm reports his imaginative young friend having made, is comparison with a studfarm. Wilhelm response is a conciliatory admission that he can be 'almost as sarcastic' as his young friend in 'hating all the idolatry practised with children', but there is, after all, much to be said for there being a 'blessing in family descent'.[117] Twelve years on, Kierkegaard is writing of all this 'seriousness and self-importance about breeding children, as though it were the meaning of life' with immortality 'one fine day' tagged on. Leaving that day to look after itself, people dote over 'family histories and family trees', counting marriages and children, with the 'priest play[ing] the stud-master'.[118] Should we not suspect that the real author is less at home in the Or than in the moods and feelings recorded and so cogently expressed in the Either? Is the Or not, in reality, just a long diversion in which private messages are sent to the lady he has wronged and with a postscript that opens the door to redemption?

The truth seems to be an In-between. Wilhelm represents an ideal of universality in his own light. It is an ideal we should all share, but the way in which we do so calls for a radical change. Those who cannot share it in its current form should not, however, suppose they are special or in any way superior, for those like the Jutland farmers whose faith has not been put to the irrelevant test of philosophy should have our respect. Perhaps we should even envy them. The difficulties faced by Christians have to do with the cultivation of spirit, understood not as cordiality, good neighbourliness, or even empathy which is something deeper, but as the self-insight that

---

117   *SKS* 3, p. 77/*Either/Or*, p. 420.
118   *SKS* 26, NB34:17, p. 329/*KJN* 10, p. 338.

any such consideration for others presupposes and, most of all, insight into the psychological and not just sociological or merely political reasons for an inability to join society on its own terms:

> *A man may have himself to blame for this imperfection, or he can have it quite blamelessly, but it can still be true that he cannot realize the universal. If people were in general more energetically self-aware then perhaps many would arrive at the same conclusion.*

The words are Wilhelm's. By presenting marriage as an ideal that few marriages actually realize, he appears to imply that the institution is for those energetic enough in their self-awareness to enter into it, but that these are just those most likely to find themselves blamelessly out of the universal's reach.[119]

In these closing pages Wilhelm appears to merge increasingly with his and his young friend's editor, and the latter with the real author. Kierkegaard at the time of writing was someone who had escaped marriage, but he wouldn't and couldn't dismiss the institution as such. One good reason was that he would have his ex-fiancée understand that she might find someone who didn't share his difficulties. Regine became engaged to her future husband just six months after *Either/Or* was published and Kierkegaard later records that he 'affirmed' her marriage 'entirely' and 'thanked God' for it.[120] More than that, he regretted not having had this way of realizing the universal at his own disposal: if only his 'wretchedness' had not got in the way, he would gladly have married his fiancée.

---

119   *SKS* 3, p. 310/*Either/Or*, p. 586.
120   *SKS* 22, NB11:183, p. 111/*KJN* 6, p. 108.

And hadn't he become the 'most inspired champion of marriage'?[121]

Spared the difficulties, Wilhelm is nevertheless made psychologist enough to see their possibility and to imagine the consequences for one who, instead of savouring exceptionality or even vaunting it, faces the universal as a 'severe master' that it is 'constantly holding the sword of justice over him', saying: 'Why do you want to be outside?' And it is no use saying 'It is not my fault', for the excluded individual is 'accountable' all the same, and the claims of justice are always there to be met.[122]

In short, there is little of Kierkegaard himself to see or hear in the way that Wilhelm defends the ethical life. But by letting him make a good case for it, a position is established from where in typical 'dialectical' fashion a case for the exception can be formed as its opposite. By projecting his own psychological acuity onto Wilhelm, Kierkegaard is able to prepare the way for his 'thesis' that God is accessible only in a singularity first properly experienced in an isolation from which it becomes evident that 'to be a Christian is to be single'.[123]

The corollary here is that from a properly Christian point of view the exception is not the one who fails to marry but marriage itself. Apart from anything else, *Either/Or*'s 'Aesthetic Validity of Marriage' (the title of the second epistle) is a way of saying that even under not very exceptional circumstances, one should not marry. In Wilhelm's closing words we see how the reader, with the universal now firmly established but the relationship to it open, is led back to the boundary where the aesthete is caught up in a potentially self-creative tension between

---

121   *SKS* NB10:200, p. 378/*SKS* 5, p. 378.
122   *SKS* 3, p. 312 /*Either/Or*, p. 588.
123   *SKS* 26, NB34:22, p. 335/*KJN* 10, p. 343.

the Scylla of a universal embedded in culture and the Charybdis of an 'I' that, like the flying predator its near namesake, the culture devours.

Isolation

Behind those three easy-reader's catchphrases or labels we find not three stages with a leap either qualifying or disqualifying the author as an existentialist thinker; rather, we tease out three intertwining threads that wind their several ways through the writing but somehow come together within the complex weave of biography: (1) a critique of a liberalist religion that hollows out the true core of a religion that should be everyone's possession; (2) a polemic carried on with intellectual skills maybe even superior to those of its targets, but which at the same time protects and perhaps consciously defends a father's less complicated but deeply entrenched faith; and (3) a literary career that excuses an exceptionality that was, in part, the son's birth-right and inheritance but when supercharged by an equally inborn polemical nature and lately discovered literary talent, helped him out of the added gift of 'congenital melancholia'.[124]

It did so by providing a theme within whose wide-ranging parameters a social miscreant with a bad conscience could, in the saving category of 'the single individual', seek redemption for having let a young lady down. It was a category he had found by becoming it himself. The fact that in carrying out these

---

124 *SKS* 22, NB11:27, p. 64/*KJN* 6, p. 19*; cf. *SKS* 23, NB17:45, p. 193/ *KJN* 7, p. 196 ('primal melancholia').

personal errands he happened to become the father of Existentialism is as unsurprising as the variety of that cult's, movement's or philosophy's many manifestations.

Of his own *curriculum vitae*, Kierkegaard writes of having 'run' through a 'series' of Or's. Under the heading 'Either/Or', he notes that this was what they had called him 'at the time'. It was when he had 'indicated marriage' as the Or, but that 'of course was not [his] life's Or'. As for his actual coordinates, these placed him 'even further away from that Either'. But there had been 'in-between' positions: gratification (the essence of the Either) with an 'ethical' additive, and another with an 'ethico-religious' additive. But neither of these was yet his own Or. So, there was,

> only one Or left: suffering, renunciation, the religious, becoming less than nothing in this world. ... If I am a dialectician by origin, if my nature is dialectics, then I can only find rest in the final Or, not in any intermediate Or; for only when repose is found in the final Or is the Either/Or exhausted.[125]

Was the repose that of one who had become as exhausted as the Either/Or? None of the worldly attachments of the Either would work even if they were there to enjoy. That could of course be a matter of physical weariness rather than spiritual birth let alone growth. But what about *spiritual* weariness? Wouldn't just the same symptoms apply? Surely, spiritual strength is a matter of staying the course, of being like Abraham, or that down-at-heel tax-collector who believed that something would turn up round every next corner?

The final entry in Kierkegaard's journals, from three

---

125   SKS 25, NB26:110, p. 104/*KJN* 9, p. 102*.

years later, suggests that he may have looked at it otherwise. It begins by saying that '[t]his life's destiny is to be brought to the highest degree of weariness with life ...The person who, brought to this point, is able to maintain — or is helped by God to be able to maintain — that it is God who, out of love, has brought him to this point: he, understood from a Christian point of view, has passed life's examination, is ripe for eternity'.[126]

The task has been accomplished, the contest with 'Either' is over, and it is now time for the reward. Kierkegaard's 'Or' catalogue had been written in 1852. That was a year after a period in more pastoral surroundings just outside the city walls and he had moved back into town. In those quieter surroundings he had written another short book, *For Self-Examination, Judge for Yourself* (*Til Selv-Prøvelse Samtiden Anbefalet*). It would not be published until twenty-one years after his death. The hermit was no longer addressing his contemporaries. The polemicist, although not *hors de combat*, was back in his tent reflecting on his 'life's operation'. He was also, in practice, writing for us. Looking at this final period more closely, we can see a new Either/Or in two alternative ways for readers themselves to judge 'for themselves' the contribution of *Either/Or*'s real author.

The fifth number of the *Moment*, published on the 27th of July, 1855, ties the situation that Kierkegaard brought upon himself to those difficult words of Luke about 'hating father, mother, one's own children, wife etc.'. An embarrassment to many Christians, these words are tactfully omitted in a virtual censorship in some versions of the sayings of Christ,[127] but Kierkegaard makes no such concession. He calls it 'the strongest

---

126   *SKS* 27, *Paper* 591, p. 696/*KJN*, 11,2, p. 405.
127   . As, e.g., in *Verba Christi: The Sayings of Christ*, Temple Classics London: J. M. Dent, 1905. Other citations have casuistically offered milder translations of the Greek '*misein*'.

expression of the most tormenting isolation'.[128] The connection is clear: the isolation is his own.

Isolation and solitude differ; you may seek solitude, while isolation is a matter of being kept out or in another way kept in. Here it was a case of keeping *himself* out (or in), and he seems to mean that he was making a point by doing so. The question posed to the reader is whether it is a good one.

To some, it may seem that the repose of the final Or he writes about is that of one who has finally given up. In the words of *Fear and Trembling* it would be 'resignation'. There, the clearance of resignation, or giving up hope, is needed to make room for the option of faith proper to stand before you. In resisting the hold that the world still has on you, faith requires strength. But here, for Kierkegaard, drained of energy, the world itself appears to have been emptied of any attraction: a personal history of effort has ended in exhaustion. Yet faith seems to have been a passenger to the end. Having now passed the examination, he has earned the eternity diploma. With no change, or possibility of either failure or achievement remaining, and no change in sight except death, he could be said, in a derivative sense, to be as close as humanly possible to the unchangeability of God.

Lying in hospital during those six weeks before he died, Kierkegaard was visited on several occasions by his trusted confidant Emil Boesen, a priest and who had to travel from Jutland to talk with his long-time

---

128   *SKS* 13, p. 234; cf. Luke 14.27: 'Whoever comes to me and does not hate father and mother, wife and children, and brothers and sisters, yes, and even life itself, cannot be my disciple'. Matt 10.37 has a milder version: 'Whosoever loves father or mother more than me is not worthy of me, and whoever loves son or daughter more than me is not worthy of me'. Both cite the same fate for those who do not 'take up the cross'.

friend. Kierkegaard's remarks reveal the mark that the polemic of self-enforced isolation had left on him. He had refused to see the journalist friend and newspaper editor who had been his go-between in publishing the pseudonymous works. Why? 'He did me personal favours but disowned me in public. That I cannot stand.' His brother was also turned away, even though he had travelled some distance from his parsonage. Why? Because not so long ago he had described Søren in public as 'ecstatic' and, by contrast, praised Hans Lassen Martensen as a model of discretion and composure.

Was Kierkegaard unforgiving? Perhaps he was simply too weary to negotiate a reconciliation in a fraught and life-long fraternal relationship. Even talking to Boesen took its toll. But then, reverting to Luke, we might wonder whether father and mother would have been turned away too? And what of Regine?

There was that assurance that if only his 'wretchedness' had not got in the way, he would gladly have married his fiancée. From his hospital bed, Kierkegaard admitted to Boesen that the *Moment* 'and all that' was now behind him. If the Luke quotation may be read as an expression of authorial ecstasy on the pamphlet editor's part, the ex-editor now had a friendlier and more 'fireside' version of the quotation to offer:

> *What matters is to get as close to God as possible. There are those who have need of others, the many, all that nonsense about large numbers of people. There is someone who has need only of one. He stands highest among those who need anyone, he who needs most stands lowest. Only one person is needed to say this.*[129]

---

129   Kirmmse, *Encounters*, pp.123-124, p. 121/*Erindringer om Søren Kierkegaard*, ed. Steen Johansen, C.A. Reitzels Forlag, Copenhagen 1980, pp 12-20/Søren Kierekgaard, *Papers and Journals: A Selection*, trans. Alastair Hannay, London 1996, p. 654.

Kierkegaard saw himself as being such a one. Unable to 'enter into ordinary relations', he had concluded that his task was 'out of the ordinary'. Yet, although 'tossed about as a plaything of [divine] Governance', he had tried to carry it out 'as best as [he] could'. That is 'always the existence and the fate of a special messenger'.[130]

In an age of random terrorism with ties to ideologies of divinity having a fairly obvious pathology, any claim to be special in this way tends to be suspect. But it is in retrospect, and not in the form of self-enlistment in a supposedly divine operation, that Kierkegaard ascribes to himself the role of special messenger, and we may agree that it has less to do with compensation for loss of social identity, and more to do with a feeling of the need to revise the terms of an identity that had always been his own. There is even some sense of averting catastrophe in that respect. A journal entry from 1849 says that '[o]ne solitary person cannot help or save an age; he can only make it clear that it is on its way to a downfall'.[131] Thinking back over his 'task', he said that it had been 'fitting, important and difficult enough'. He reminded Boesen that he had 'seen things from the very core of Christianity, while everything is postponement, postponement, all of it, simply putting things off. ...'

Asked if he would take the last rites, Kierkegaard replied that it could only be from a layman. Where no one can die without the blessing of one of those 'thousand priests' who dish out Christianity to all those who want everything so 'comfortably arranged', it is not God but they 'who are sovereign ...'. Priests were

---

130   Kirmmse, *Encounters with Kierkegaard*, p. 121; for the source see p.304. The Danish, 'det er altid de extraordinære Sendebuds Tilværelse og Skjebne' can also be translated, 'it is always the life and lot of the special messengers'. See *Papers and Journals: A Selection*, pp. 651 and 654.

131   *SKS* 21, NB10:93, p. 304/*KJN* 5, p. 314.

only 'royal functionaries' and had 'nothing to do with Christianity'.[132]

As death approached, the 'repose' of that final Or described above may, for all we know, have been closer in mood to some more wistful words quoted six years earlier and in quite another tone, but also quoting Christ. They tell us to be 'like' those lilies and birds, for they 'neither toil nor spin' nor do they 'sow'.[133] Freed from the worries that give rise to our unending questions of moral principle and choice, and unhampered by thoughts of yesterday and tomorrow, these creatures offer *images* of what it is to be following God's will with unalloyed joy. For what, after all, is it 'to be joyful?'.

> *It is truly to be present to oneself; but truly to be present to oneself is this 'today', this to be today, truly to be today. And the truer it is that you are today, the more you are entirely present to yourself in being today, the less does tomorrow, the day of misfortune, exist for you. Joy is the present time, with the entire emphasis falling on the present time.*

That is why God, who 'eternally says: "Today" ... is blessed' and 'eternally and infinitely present to himself in being today'. It is also why 'the lily and the bird are joy', because 'by silence and unconditional obedience they are entirely present to themselves in being today'.[134]

Here, the challenge is not, as in Luke, to dim the world's appeal by switching focus onto an unchanging God under whose sovereign shadow all else becomes secondary: it is to look at your own life here on earth and everything around you as if it were for *you*,

---

132   *Papers and Journals: A Selection*, p. 655.
133   Matt 6:25–34.
134   *SKS* 11, 43/ *The Lily of the Field and the Bird of the Air*, trans. Bruce H. Kirmmse, Princeton, 2016, p. 77.

> *that you came into existence, that you exist, that 'today' you receive the necessities of existence, that you came into existence, that you became a human being, that you can see [...] hear [...] have a sense of smell [...] a sense of taste, that you can feel; that the sun shines for you and for your sake [...] that spring comes, that birds come in large flocks — and do so in order to bring you joy [...]: If this is nothing to rejoice over, then there is nothing over which to rejoice.*[135]

A disposition to rejoice is not a card we would expect to be dealt to someone later claiming congenital melancholia; its manifestations are something that a true melancholic can surely do nothing but imagine, although the ability to do so and the need are no doubt a source of much great art and literature. A deathbed, on the other hand, may offer something as close as need be to savouring what it means to be no more than 'today'. Might not the repose that Kierkegaard talks of be that of someone no longer plagued by those causes of regret and hopes for the future that prevent such an experience? Once acknowledged, even regrets can be laid to rest when further repairs to the past are no longer possible. The conditions of existence itself may even be said to slip away, leaving one as close as can be to a sense of the eternal of the kind evoked in music by the repeated *'evig'* in the closing bars of the *Abschied* in Gustav Mahler's *Das Lied von der Erde*. The Earth, so long as we let it last, is still there for others. Instead of the repetitive coming and going of the seasons envisaged by Johannes *de silentio* in *Fear and Trembling*, there is this natural world whose naturalness is offered to humans

---

135   *SKS* 11, 43-44/*The Lily of the Field and the Bird of the Air*, pp. 78-79.

as an image of the joy they otherwise achieve only by self-deception. It is an eternity that only self-aware creatures can appreciate and an image of joy possible only for beings indelibly prone to its opposite.

Model misfits

It seems that life for Kierkegaard had to be a task. In his own culture, and officially in ours too, this has for many centuries not been the only way of grasping the situation we find ourselves in. It has also been presented to us as a gift to make the most of as long as it lasts. A more banal version has it as an opportunity to grasp and make the most of while we can. Both of these fail to mention the social part of the task. Ideally, we might all get along with each other and have no more problems than ants engaged in the concerted activity of building an anthill. More likely, however, given human nature and its situation, treating life as something presented on a tray to pick and choose from, and from whose resources to make the most of for ourselves, is to invite self-annihilating conflict.

Kierkegaard noted in his dissertation that the gift is to be seen *as* a task.[136] The isolation that became his way of life can be a dangerous place for those seeking a task to make something of themselves: solitude breeds belief in a messianic calling, some *idée fixe* that might take many directions. But if the idea of being allotted a personal task may be born *of* isolation, in Kierkegaard's case it may be

---

136   SKS 1, *Begrebet Ironi*, pp. 312 and 315/*The Concept of Irony*, trans. Howard V. Hong and Edna H. Hong, Princeton, 1989, pp. 276-277 and 279. The Danish 'opgave' can also mean 'problem', 'puzzle', and also 'school exercise', implying not just a job to do but a problem to be solved..

better seen as a matter of being born *to* it. From early on he had sought out — or perhaps in his wide reading happily came across — models in the cultural wardrobe of figures, real or fictional, whose lives went against the stream. One of these was Don Juan in the guise of Mozart's Don Giovanni, He earned a place in *Either/Or* as an exponent of the third 'immediate erotic stage' of the aesthetic life.[137] There was also Ahasuerus, the Wandering Jew, with his 'life' sentence until Doomsday for taunting Jesus on the way to the crucifixion. That inveterate trickster Till Eulenspiegel, the hero of many typically irreverent folktales, was also on the list. In Kierkegaard's long-drawn out student days, that middle-class breaker of bourgeois taboos, Faust also came out of the identity wardrobe on a brief but serious visitation. Not least there was, and it could be argued lastingly, the legendary Master Thief,[138] the renegade whose belief in his better grasp of society and its ills emboldened him to risk his life in challenging the *status quo*. There is a link here to the Socrates, who took hemlock rather than seek refuge in exile, as his friends had urged when he was convicted of corrupting youth and not following the state religion. Both outsiders planned to convince their judges that it was they who were in the wrong.

These form shades on a spectrum of non-conformity from hopeless exclusion to that sense of superior insight that led Kierkegaard to imagine the Danish primate would join forces with him, though no doubt with a proviso that as subjective thinkers they could never be *seen* to support each other, nor even see each other as such.

These were all early heroes. Recognition came late to another, although the credentials were already there in *Fear and Trembling*. It was seven years after its publication that Kierkegaard came to describe Abraham

---

[137]   *SKS* 2, pp. 89 ff./*Either/Or*, pp. 93 ff.
[138]   *SKS* 27, Paper 97:2, p. 119/*KJN* 3, *Notebook* 2, pp. 85-91.

as the 'eternal prototype' of the genuinely religious person:

> *As he had to leave the land of his forefathers for a foreign land, so indeed must the religious person leave, i.e., forsake, an entire generation of his contemporaries — even though he remains among them, albeit isolated, alien to them. Being an alien, being in exile — this is precisely the characteristic suffering of the religious person.*[139]

Less a matter of living as if destined for a better world than the one he lived in, the faith Kierkegaard himself breathes is for this world. It may sound like that of someone hanging grimly onto an inherited trust in its ability to produce a joy that he repeatedly tells us was never, or only very briefly, his. What we read sounds less like someone taking a chance on better things to come, than a desperate (hence not yet despairing) pressing on in the face of doubt about his own motives and achievements. It is the unwavering trust of an Abraham that rings more truly, with the father of Isaac believing the 'absurd' as he rides silently up the mountain with his son.[140] The image had been one that Kierkegaard noted down in a draft sermon even before *Fear and Trembling*. He had written:

> *We ought [to] attend particularly to this trusting God-devoted disposition, to this cheerful and unhesitating willingness to face trials, to answer bravely: Here I am.*[141]

---

139   *SKS* 23, NB18:64, p. 96/*KJN* 7, p. 300.
140   *SKS* 4, pp. 114 and 117/*Fear and Trembling*, pp. 51 and 54.
141   *SKS* 18, HH:8, p. 29/*KJN* 2, p. 121.

As with Abraham and Job, the trials Kierkegaard faced were not intellectual. His fight was with academics who talked religion but lived in a world where everything 'is' and nothing 'becomes'.[142] A tireless thinker himself, subjective at that, and one who insisted that it was the 'single individual' who was 'in the medium of becoming',[143] his restless mind deprived him of that ability to 'live for today'. That could be why he especially treasured its possibility. He says that in writing the *Lily of the Field and the Bird of the Air* he was not 'fighting with anybody' or 'speaking about myself'.[144]

---

142   See *SKS* 7, 1, pp. 21 ff./*CUP*, pp. 159 ff.
143   *SKS* 21, NB8:75, p. 176/*KJN* 5, p. 184.
144   *SKS.* 21, NB10:169, pp. 340-341/*KJN* 8, p. 352.

Delivery dues

The journal entry on being ready to back up his writing in 'the most decisive manner', where Kierkegaard allows that a 'dash of pride' had found its way into his melancholia but now 'everything was as it should be', went on to say:

> *As the poet's song echoes with a sigh from his own unhappy love; so too will all my inspired talk about the ideal of being a Christian echo with a sigh: Alas! I am not a Christian, I am only a Christian poet and thinker.*[145]

We may be reminded of *The Sorrows of Young Werther*, but as contrast, not comparison. Although Goethe's hero's love was here on earth, it shone with the romantic glow and intensity of the eternal. He took his own life not as a martyr sacrificing himself even in a 'lesser sense', but as the victim of an unresolvable love affair. Kierkegaard was also involved in a threesome, but the other two were now happily married and Kierkegaard kept his attachment at a distance. The young Kierkegaard's initial sorrows had been over another loss, that of the 'few dear departed' at a time when he was in desperate need of a self-organizing selfhood. That came by way of the 'task' of salvaging a form strong enough to provide an excuse

---

145   *SKS* 21, NB10:200, pp. 368-369/*KJN* 5, pp. 378-379.

for breaking a vow of marriage. The sorrow here was sweetened by the discovery, during the relationship, of a hitherto academically stifled literary talent. The newly found gift allowed him to present his own dilemma in so many imaginative ways, but then came another period of anguish as he fought the creeping suspicion that, for all his pious thoughts, it had been to his own benefit all along.

During the period of those first pseudonyms, Kierkegaard had dedicated his signed discourses to his 'dear reader'. He tells us later that the addressee was not you or me, but Regine. When looking back over his authorship from a firmly established religious perspective, he was now on the lookout for a generally applicable unifying principle that he might bring to the world in general. It was something the lack of which he had always criticized in others and all those years earlier had anxiously sought in his own person. He thought he had found it in the 'category of the single individual', introduced in the *Point of View for my Work as Author*, a book published posthumously by his older brother.

Kierkegaard writes there of the category having been granted him by circumstances that were divinely appointed. Until then it had only been recognized as a manner of speech, which is 'why it still strikes people as self-regarding and presuming to talk of the single individual, while in fact this is exactly what absolute humanity is: namely that everyone is a single individual'. It sounds like a privilege, but as soon as you try to be one, you will see it requires 'ethical [and] religious courage'.[146] This 'category' is the one 'through which in a religious sense the time), history itself and the human race must pass'.[147] In his journal he writes:

---
146   *SKS* 20, NB:123, p. 88/*KJN* 4, NB, p. 87*.
147   *SKS*.20, NB3:77, p. 280/*KJN* 4, p. 280.

If only this was the right category, if what was said about it was in order, if I perceived it correctly and understood properly that this was my task . . . then I stand and my writings with me.[148]

'Two Notes' is included at the end of *The Point of View*. There the single individual is presented as the thread connecting the earlier pseudonyms with the later works. Readers of the earlier works wondering where that thread begins, would, as we noted, find it at the end of *Either/Or*'s over seven hundred pages. Even the careful reader may find those final comments too tightly presented to pause over. What, after all, can be added after a minor court judge has himself spent over three hundred pages in two long epistles telling his wayward young friend that marriage is the way to pull himself together and present a visibly dependable self to the world?

That this was not just the polemical stance handed to a pseudonymous hireling is indicated in a journal entry four years after *Either/Or*. It says that the 'second part begins with marriage because that is the most profound form of the revelation of life'.[149] This was the Or that he had abandoned before leaving for Berlin to write about its advantages.

Wilhelm, in his role of judge a civic official, talks of his own marriage and speaks of 'realizing' or 'accomplishing' what in English translation is usually referred to as the 'universal'. The text has *'det Almene'* which, as equivalent to the German '*Allgemeine*', was a term that Kierkegaard would link with the vocabulary of German Idealism. This,

---
148 Ibid.
149 *Papirer* IV A 234, (not presently found in *SKS* or *KJN*) see *Papers and Journals: A Selection*, p. 165.

as his more perceptive readers would quickly realize, was the way of thinking that Kierkegaard's 'single individual' was designed to undermine. In its everyday application, we can think of notions like seemliness and decency, responsibility and reliability. We convey it with expressions such as 'the right thing to do', 'not letting the side down', 'in the public or [and nearer the original sense] common interest'. Failure to 'realize' or 'accomplish the universal would be expressed in words like 'unseemly', 'anti-social', 'maverick', 'nogoodnik', etc. We also have 'dropouts' and 'misfits' and a wide range of the socially invisible, from dangerous 'sociopaths' to the less profiled 'black sheep' and 'dark horse'.

The latter metaphor may capture the sense in which Wilhelm takes failure to accomplish the universal to be a matter of social invisibility. His young friend is socially obscure in the sense that he fails to *disclose* a through-time self to be relied on in virtue of resource and social status. The special virtue of marriage, if properly undertaken, is exactly its open and clear disclosure of such a self. The married person (here emphatically the man) becomes the visible occupant of an essential role that keeps society intact and in marriage arranges for its seemly continuation. Failure to come into the open in this and similar ways, according to what Wilhelm has learned and now teaches his young friend, is to waste one's life in a series of whims and satisfactions for which the world has to supply the occasion, and which as the palate becomes jaded by over-stimulation becomes a diminishing resource. It is to remain ever more desperately in the passive and opportunist role of one who seizes chances, whether for pleasure or whatever more refined forms of satisfaction, even or especially those of 'self'-advancement, turn up, or can be conjured from the surroundings. Any 'improvement' of the self, in its own eyes, that fails to look beyond personal satisfactions and ignores the 'universal' or common weal is, for Wilhelm and surely also for Kierkegaard, not yet a self.

As noted, having made a strong case for realizing the universal in a socially recognizable way, in just one and a half pages Wilhelm leaves his young friend with the thought of another way of realizing the universal, a concealed way open to one who is 'uncommon' and where social identity is not the crucial criterion but with the universal still somehow operative as a goal. Wilhelm's imagined exception feels the strain of not joining in and understands the ignominy of being despised for not doing the common thing. Wilhelm says: 'He will feel that the upbringing that has fallen to his lot is hard, for the universal is a severe master when one has it outside one.' But, from the side-lines of society, the exception will 'rejoice in the others to whom it has been granted to accomplish this thing', but then also 'see perhaps better than they do how beautiful it is ...'.[150]

Now, twenty-years after that summer recreation when orientation beyond the limits of time and space had seemed not only a good idea but essential to his sense, not just of well-being, but also of being himself at all, the beauty of the universal would seem more whimsy than a quality regrettably absent from the universal as he now saw himself related to it. The burden of that defence of the ethical had, after all, been borne by claims about the 'aesthetic validity' of marriage, its appeal to a satisfied and aesthetically satisfying selfhood. But, now that he had 'seen things from the very core of Christianity', aesthetic considerations were no part of his own relationship to the universal.

---

150   *SKS* 3, pp. 311-313/*Either/Or*, pp. 588-589.

And what about God? For Wilhelm, the divine was not accessible in the way that God, subsequently, had come close to Kierkegaard personally, if not as another person but as 'subject' to one who by becoming a single self was also now 'subject'. Is there not then reason to suppose that the hidden import of the special messenger's message is that the aesthete has a better chance than the ethicist of coming close to God?

When it comes to cultivating spirit, once all culture has been scorned as a matrix on which selfhood is formed without remainder, the limbo of the ironist's own emptily 'superior' position is where we are most likely to form a view of the divine that answers to the kinds of need that Kierkegaard writes about, and which his writings increasingly express.

It is a matter of interpretation, but there are numerous passages in the 'Either' part of 'Either/Or' that are not only wrung from the writer's desolate heart, but which in retrospect show an uncanny prescience of what was to come. Several passages offer readers a chance to form and face their own interpretative Either/Or's. Here is one, in a piece entitled in 'Ancient Tragedy's Reflection in the Modern':

> *The tragic contains an infinite leniency; really it is what divine love and mercy are, but from the aesthetic perspective on human life; it is even milder, and so I would say it was a maternal love which soothes the troubled. The ethical is strict and harsh. So, if a criminal pleads to the judge that his mother had a propensity for stealing, and particularly at the time she was carrying him, the judge secures the Board of Health's opinion of his mental*

> condition and decides that what he is dealing
> with is a thief and not a thief's mother. Since
> we are talking about a crime, the sinner can't
> very well flee to the temple of aesthetics, and
> yet the aesthetic will put in an extenuating
> word for him. Still, it would be wrong for him
> to seek comfort there, for his path leads him
> not to the aesthetic but the religious. .... The
> religious is the expression of a paternal love,
> since it contains the ethical but in a mollified
> form. And mollified by what? Precisely by what
> gives the tragic the leniency: continuity.[151]

Two opposites, leniency and harshness, are allied to another pair, mother and father, and both to aesthetics and religion. The lenient mother takes the reason for grief from out of the griever's hands, while the harsh father follows the Board of Health's advice. The aesthete who purportedly wrote this had admittedly not yet read Wilhelm's letters, but a question to be asked is, would they bring him closer to the Kierkegaard who found himself closer to God? And, of course, Kierkegaard wrote the letters and the reflections of the one yet to receive them. That raises another question. What ties, or threads, are there still to detect between Kierkegaard the child who sorrowed so deeply over the death of his lenient mother and found in his own father the meaning of God's fatherly love, and this self-exiled polemicist who has seen what he took to be Christianity from its suffering core?

That his father was never far from his mind is clear to the last. There is the comment from that 'bad' year 1848 that the 'best proof of the immortality of the soul, for the existence of God, etc. is the impression one gets of this

---

151   SKS 2, p. 145/*Either/Or*, p. 145.

in one's childhood and is therefore the proof that, unlike those many learned and pretentious proofs, could be put like this: It is certainly true, because my father told it to me'.[152]

The quotation and timing bring together some scattered facts from along the way. Kierkegaard had said that it was his father that gave him a glimpse of *God's fatherly love*.[153] His early childhood or lack of it and his upbringing seem never to have deserted him, or he it. In 1849 he reminds himself and us of how as a child he was told that Christ even though he was the 'truth' was 'spat on'.[154] But, as for his own suffering, the father's faith could help here too:

> I owe everything to my father from the very beginning. When, melancholic as he was, he saw melancholy in me, his plea was: See to it that you truly love Jesus Christ.[155]

Just a year earlier, the point of focus out of time and space from that reflective summer of 1835 comes up again:

> The Archimedean point beyond the world is the place of prayer where one who truly prays, prays in all honesty: and he will move the earth. Yes, if he really exists, this person who prays truly, when he shuts the door it is unbelievable what he achieves.[156]

It seems, then, that the solitary person, the single individual, achieves this singularity not just by focusing *on* a point beyond the constraints of time and space',

---

152   *SKS* 20, NB5:114, p. 417/*KJN* 4, p. 418*.
153   *SKS* 19, Notebook 6:24, p. 200/*KJN* 3, p. 196.
154   *SKS* 21, NB10:191, p. 356/*KJN* 4, p. 368.
155   *SKS* 20, NB5:65, p. 399/*KJN* 4, p. 400.
156   *SKS* 20, NB5:111, p. 416/*KJN* 4, p. 417.

but by closing the doors on time and space and actually occupying that point. In geometrical terms, a point has neither length, width, nor breadth. That suggests that in our singularity, which begins with the ironist's emptied self, we are to reach beyond our bodily and encultured selves to a universal but abstract pole whose universal message can nevertheless only be deciphered in a language we learn from each other. Christians, however, have an example to follow, one whose credentials as exemplar defy understanding and whose eternal divinity they take for granted and can express only in words that won't work within a common vocabulary.

On his sole visit to Sæding in East Jutland, where the Kierkegaard family had its origins, Søren wrote of the heathland there. It was here, his father had once told his sons, that as a twelve-year-old watching sheep he had in his misery cursed God. As he saw it, Kierkegaard the heath 'must be peculiarly suited to developing spiritual strength'.

> [H]ere everything lies naked and unveiled before God, and there is no place here for all those distractions, the many nooks and crannies in which consciousness can take cover and from which seriousness often has difficulty catching up with distracted thoughts. Here consciousness has to take a firm and precise grip on itself. 'Whither shall I flee from thy presence?' is something one can truly say on the heath.[157]

---

157 *SKS* 19, Notebook 6:29, p. 201/*KJN* 3, p. 197; cf. Patrick Stokes, *The Naked Self: Kierkegaard and Personal Identity*, Oxford, 2015, where Kierkegaard's relevance for contemporary philosophical disputes on identity is fully discussed.

The home that Michael Pedersen Kierkegaard was to provide for his family was not far from being a domestic version of that same landscape. There was no escaping God's presence here either. Just as a twelve-year-old out on the heath could only curse and not deny God, so as mentioned earlier was a 41-year-old sophisticate born in Copenhagen able to note in his journal that feeling ignored by God was the 'most fearful of all [of God's] punishments'.[158] Through an interesting twist of this negative theology, if praying to God could never alter the unchangeable Deity,[159] at least opening the door was an invitation to the unchangeable Deity to come back and show some interest again. That, however, on Kierkegaard's view, should be read as an interest on the part of the one who prays in changing for the better.

The talk that Kierkegaard gave on God's immutability (*Guds Uforanderlighed*) on the 5th of May 1854 was published in the *Moment* on the 1st of August 1855 with a dedication to the memory of 'my late father, Michael Pedersen Kierkegaard'.

---

158   *SKS* 26, NB 34:25, p. 337/*KJN* 3, p. 346.
159   *SKS* 8, p. 137/*Upbuilding Discourses in Various Spirits*, trans. Howard V. Hong and Edna H. Hong, Princeton, 1993, p. 22.

The dealt hand

The family name, like so many others in Jutland, had been Pedersen. To identify a Pedersen out of context you had to mention a homestead or occupation. The family tended the farmland belonging to the church in a sparsely inhabited district in Jutland called Sæding. A 'kirkegaard' might be a regular farm ('gaard) attached to the church, but as in the parish of Sæding it also took in the graveyard with the church (*kirk*) at its centre.

Michael Pedersen Kierkegaard's religious roots went deeper than farming the parish lands. His son Søren, following a confession by his then over eighty-year-old father, was to write in his journal of the 'dreadful thought' of the 'small boy, who tending sheep on the Jutland heath, in much suffering, and starving and exhausted, stood up on a hill and cursed God'.[160] By the time he was forty-two years old, the intelligent young Jutland shepherd had become a rich merchant in Copenhagen. He had been exposed in his youth to the influence of the Moravian Brotherhood, also called Herrnhuters (the word 'Herrnhut' meaning 'the lord's protection'), following their arrival in South Jutland in the 1770s. This evangelical sect had been established in Bohemia in the eighteenth century and was dedicated to keeping the Christian message alive in a world that was losing touch with its ideals. The Brothers were known for their

---

160   *SKS* 8, JJ:416, p. 278/*KJN* 2, p. 257.

artisan and merchandizing skills, and in their pietistic approach they looked down on a liberal theology for which being religious was to know the right words and agree to them. It was also out of tune with the populist Grundtvigians, for whom being religious was essentially a congregational get-together.[161] The Moravians brought something new to both of these. They gave people in outlying areas a sense of being part of something universal that the fashionable new approaches denied them. By the time that the former shepherd boy had reached the age of forty-two, the Moravians had come to the city and in Copenhagen they were numerous enough to need a larger meeting place. With his accumulated wealth, Michael Pedersen was able to help substantially in financing it. He could now live off his investments and devote himself to the upbringing of his children.

Why should a married man with a steady business do that? There were several reasons. Michael Pedersen's second wife had been the maid of a first wife who died childless. Ane was an unsophisticated woman and Michael Pedersen considered her unsuited to bringing up their children and chose to take on that task himself. Retirement also gave him an opportunity to give himself the education he had never received as a child. He started reading German philosophy. which he would then discuss with his sons. Michael Pedersen took charge of the household, including buying the food, leaving Ane with the tasks of a nanny.

In order to give his children a less confined and more socially acceptable religious background, a regime of church-going that went beyond his own Moravian background was established. Søren, the youngest child,

---

[161] Nikolaj Frederik Severin Grundtvig was responsible for the *folkhøyskole* tradition and he and his followers saw Christianity in the light of a fruition of the Nordic heritage.

was born when his father was already fifty-five and was thus more exposed than his siblings to his father's late re-creation of himself. In sharing his father's lively imagination, he seems to be the most receptive to the father's attentions.

By the time Søren had reached the age of twenty-one, two of his three brothers had died, one after a schoolyard accident and the other from tuberculosis after emigrating to the United States. His two sisters, one of them his favourite, had died in childbirth in their early thirties. By then, his mother was also dead. The loss of this gentle and kindly woman reportedly left Søren inconsolable. Typical, however, of the now witty and sharp-tongued young man he had become, no direct word of the mother or her death is to be found in his writing. On Michael Pedersen's death, four years later, however, we learn in clear print that it was from his own father that Søren had learned the nature of God's 'fatherly' love. What the loss of motherly love meant for the future in this connection is open to surmise.

In Søren's mind the paternal love he felt went so far as to include the idea that the father had died for his son, a sacrifice made so that 'something might still come of me'.[162]

He had been living in the family's large and centrally situated family home under the shadow of a clever and successful but less imaginative older brother. Peter Christian was the son who fulfilled his father's expectations, the family's investment so to speak, while in order to escape the theocratic suffocation of his home, Søren sought refuge in Copenhagen's streets and coffee houses. By this time a familiar figure to be seen talking eagerly with friends, both on and off the street, he had

---

162   *SKS* 17, DD:126, p. 258/*KJN* 1, p. 249*.

spent seven student years taking courses in everything, including physics and mathematics, except the theology on which he was supposed to focus. Now, in order to satisfy his father's hopes, and perhaps to save his own conscience, he took up his theological studies in feverish haste and passed his theology finals. He visits his family roots in Jutland and with his mind on a normal solution to life's problems, makes advances to Regine with marriage in view. They became engaged, she then eighteen years old to his own twenty-seven. The inevitable break was delayed while he worked on his dissertation on irony 'with continual reference to Socrates', the Greek street philosopher made famous for his skill in pressing thoughts out of people in the informal debates handed down to us in Plato's Dialogues. By then he had preached the sermon required of his postgraduate degree.

Instead of pursuing the expected academic career now open to him, or entering the priesthood as his brother had hoped and expected, not least on behalf of the family's reputation, Søren left Copenhagen for Berlin. Ostensibly it was to listen to some well-advertised lectures by the German philosopher Schelling, once a student comrade of Hegel but now a critic. He attended these and also other lectures. From there began the writing for which he is famous.

A month earlier, he had scandalized his brother and Copenhagen society by ending the year-long engagement to the young lady with whom he was never to lose his attachment. Leaving her is also spoken of in terms of sacrifice, hers in terms of personal slight, and his in those of the conventional and settled future he says he would have liked to be able to choose. In an important way it had also been a godsend. Kierkegaard's prose before their meeting bore the deadening imprint of his classical learning. Once the floodgates of imagination opened and the range of his own possibilities thus widened, he could see a future outside a marriage that would have been disastrous for both. *Either/Or* was a 'script' that became the nucleus of an authorship in which the role and status of the common rule comes under scrutiny, and which in its various guises and contexts provides the authorship with its underlying theme of a searching and suffering individual to whom the common rule shuts its gates but, in doing so, offers chances for new perspectives — also for the common rule.

The turbulent mood in which Kierkegaard left Copenhagen can be felt in a series of notebook entries that he had made in that tense year following his visit to the family roots in Jutland. One of them goes like this:

> *Next to taking off every stitch of clothing, owning nothing in the world, not the least little thing, and then hurling myself into the water, nothing pleases me more than speaking a foreign language, preferably a living one, in order to become quite foreign to myself.*[163]

---

163   *SKS* 19, Notebook 7:11, p. 209 /*KJN* 3, p. 205.

Timely afterthoughts

As an 'atheist Jew' the cultural historian Georg Brandes, Kierkegaard's younger compatriot and first biographer, was another misfit who found his way to Berlin. From there he wrote to Nietzsche of having found 'one of the profoundest psychologists to be met with anywhere'.[164] The pronouncer of God's death, having by then lost his mind, was in no position to respond. But on reading *Ecce Homo* Brandes will have found *himself* described as a psychologist to be reckoned with. He had lectured in Denmark on Nietzsche, and 'what German university could you go to today to hear lectures on my philosophy[?]'.[165]

The Death of God left Nietzsche hammering out his own evolving paradigm of health and wholeness in seeming contrast to Kierkegaard's unrelenting hold on traditional holiness. He did so in a vocabulary of elevation and light that brought the human out of slavery in a way that can bring to mind the prisoners coming up from a dungeon as in Beethoven's *Fidelio*, except that for Nietzsche the darkness down there would be a metaphor for a civilization where people eked out

---

164 Georg Brandes, *Søren Kierkegaard: En kritisk Fremstilling i Grundrids* [A Critical Exposition in Outline], Copenhagen 1877, p. 107; see *Selected Letters of Friedrich Nietzsche*, ed. Oscar Levy, trans Anthony M. Ludovici, 1st. ed. New York, 1921, p. 325.

165 Friedrich Nietzsche, *The Anti-Christ, Ecce Homo, Twilight of the Idols, and Other Writings*, ed. Aaron Ridley and Judith Norman, trans. Judith Norman, Cambridge, 2005, p. 143.

their all-too-mediocre lives in subjection to religion. His promise to them was in the challenge that '[a]nyone who knows how to breathe the air of my writings will know that it is the air of high places'.[166]

Both writers used art as filters to portray society from their distinctively singular experiences and the language can be surprisingly similar. Listen, for example, to the first of *Either/Or*'s opening 'Diapsalmata'. It describes the unhappy man as one 'who hides deep anguish in his heart, but whose lips are so formed that when the sigh and cry pass through them, it sounds like lovely music',[167] and then to Nietzsche's Zarathustra who intones 'Once you had wild dogs in your cellar, but ultimately they transformed into birds and lovely singers'.[168]

Both Kierkegaard and Nietzsche gave readers, in the form of indirect autobiography, an opportunity to glimpse the real writer or his self-image through or behind their literary presentations. It isn't surprising, for example, that an echo of the take-it-or-leave-it-as-you-find-it of *Postscript*'s revocation is to be heard in Nietzsche asking readers to 'lose' him in order to find themselves.[169] But the literary surface can be slippery when the text purports to tell readers something to their advantage. What authority has the writer? Who do he or she think they are? Kierkegaard has his most didactic pseudonym assure the reader that he is 'a quite ordinary human being just like anyone else'[170] and on his death-bed he tells Boesen that he was 'no better than the others', as

---

166   Friedrich Nietzsche, *The Anti-Christ, Ecce Homo, Twilight of the Idols, and Other Writings*, p. 72.
167   *SKS* 2, 27/*Either/Or*, p. 43.
168   Friedrich Nietzsche, *Thus Spoke Zarathustra*, ed. Adrian Del Caro and Robert Pippin, Cambridge, 2006, p. 25.
169   *The Anti-Christ, Ecce Homo, Twilight of the Idols, and Other Writings*, p. 73.
170   See note 29.

well, if less convincingly, as having never said 'anything else'.[171] Nietzsche had in some ways more to disavow. Speaking through Zarathustra he could be mistaken for identifying himself with the prophet himself and readers might wonder whether the personal Nietzsche would have them believe that he was actually up there on the sunlit heights. In *Ecce Homo*'s final chapter, 'Why I am a Destiny', he writes in answer to his own question 'Have I been understood?': 'I have not said anything that I would not have said five years ago through the mouth of Zarathustra.'[172] Surely, to speak through that medium must be to present oneself as something of a prophet? Did Nietzsche really see himself in that guise?

If so, his position would differ significantly from that implicit in Kierkegaard's claim to have seen the 'core of Christianity' in the suffering of his own partly self-imposed isolation. Instead of telling fellow sufferers to have faith in the teacher whose own message offers comfort, Nietzsche would be impersonating the teacher. To tout superiority with any authority is to assume superior credentials, in this case an elevated perspective and a talent to speak convincingly both from and about it. True enough, Nietzsche too talks of suffering, but it is something that he has Zarathustra speak of as the inevitably dark background out of which light and elevation emerge.[173]

But just as the suffering real author of *Either/Or* and its successors came to see that he was not the world-denying Christian of his writings, so too was Nietzsche aware of the dangers of associating an insomniac poet

---

171 Kirmmse, *Encounters*, pp.123-124, p. 121/*Erindringer om Søren Kierkegaard*, ed. Steen Johansen, C.A. Reitzels Forlag, Copenhagen 1980, pp 12-20/*Papers and Journals: A Selection*, London 1996, p. 653.
172 Ibid., p. 150.
173 E.g. *Thus Spoke Zarathustra*, p. 22.

with the public image of a great visionary writer. Making that connection would be unnecessarily intrusive. *Ecce Homo* records the tortured history of his own Zarathustrian coming into being, but behind it sat the actual Friedrich wrapped in an overcoat and scarf with opium and chloral hydrate on hand to ease his stomach cramps and help with sleep. *Thus Spoke Zarathustra* does indeed speak of the sickly body, but presents it as an excuse used by the religious to preach of 'hinterworlds' where sickness has no place, while 'the healthy body' speaks '[m]ore honestly and more purely'.[174] There is a hint of autobiography here but bodily sickness is hardly the only form of suffering from which the light and elevation of the superior person (*Übermensch*) are supposed to emerge. Something more must lie behind Zarathustra's saying that '[c]reating — that is the great redemption from suffering, and life's becoming light.'[175]

Nietzsche clearly felt himself exposed to the dangers of biography. At one point he found that solitude had left him in a state of 'profound suspicion' by depriving him of his 'shelters' in this respect. He had therefore 'artificially to enforce, falsify and invent a suitable fiction for [him]self'.[176] It kept enough of Nietzsche in the text to be able to explain or justify and even applaud the creative vision of sunlit heights as a product of his *own* art and experience, but without the fine images being traced back to an insomniac. We might say that, as with Kierkegaard, it was the message that mattered, not the messenger, except that Kierkegaard seems willing to have others see the messenger as a token of what he had written about. Although ostensibly speaking of

---

174   *Thus Spoke Zarathustra*, p. 22.
175   *Thus Spoke Zarathustra*, p. 66.
176   Friedrich Nietzsche, *Human, All Too Human*, p. 5.

other artists, Nietzsche's remark that 'the most vigorous part of our culture is engulfed by all the learned dust of biography and compelled by the torture instruments of historical criticism to answer a thousand impertinent questions'[177] is easily referred to the man himself, who would rather that readers kept their eyes focused on Zarathustra.

If Nietzsche himself did not reach the sunlit heights presented to his readers with such sarcasm, humour, and wisdom, these latter qualities were something his work shared with that of his predecessor. It is understandable that they each shared an admiration for Schopenhauer, although in Kierkegaard's case this did not extend to the ascetic and elitist tendencies in Schopenhauer. What he liked was the 'well-aimed abuse' and those 'incomparably coarse' remarks on people who lived off philosophy by teaching it.[178]

Kierkegaard and Nietzsche were both, as this suggests, highly combative. Kierkegaard confessed to being 'polemical by nature', but Nietzsche went further and said he was 'by nature warlike'.[179] So it is hardly surprising that they also shared a taste for explosive metaphors. Nietzsche, thinking of his art rather than his insomnia, claimed to *be* 'dynamite'.[180] Kierkegaard nine year after *Either/Or* writes of having had a pseudonym plant that charge for him. Placed deep enough, by 'making room' for 'either-or' it could 'blow apart' this 'whole mess' of 'both-ands', which with its worthless Christian tag-end has a distinct tendency in 'this 'fortunate little country' to 'deify mediocrity'.[181]

---

177 See *Untimely Meditations*, p. 97.
178 *SKS* 25, NB29:95, p. 355/*KJN* 9, p. 358.
179 Ibid., p. 82: 'Ich bin meiner Art nach kriegerisch.'
180 Ibid., p. 144.
181 *SKS* 25, NB 26:112, 105-106/*KJN* 9, p. 103.

In *Ecce Homo* Nietzsche writes of his *Daybreak* as being his only book to 'end with an "Or?"'.[182] Unlike that lengthy Or due to Wilhelm, and as the question mark indicates, this one merely intimates a promised new day for which its Either has prepared the way without the 'slightest scent of gunpowder',[183] a remark that may remind us of another made by Kierkegaard in connection with writing *The Lily of the Field and the Bird of the Air*, where he was not 'fighting with anybody' or 'speaking about myself'.[184] If, as was suggested, the 'dialectic' role of the Or in *Either/Or* is to be found in those few closing and, one could also say questioning hints of a noble exceptionality, the parallel extends this far too.

A fault line, a true Either/Or, does nevertheless separate the works of these two creatively thinking writers. Nietzsche was occupied with metaphors of elevation and light and his view was from the window, in actuality often that of the Alps, while Kierkegaard wrote from the depths with the resources to be tapped there in his own person. One way of putting it would be to say that where Kierkegaard saw the self-serving mechanisms of the less than conscious mind making things look easier than they were, for Nietzsche they were there to make the world our own. In *Untimely Meditations* those less than conscious processes produced the 'illusions' without which all 'great things would never succeed'. They are there to break down a chilling sobriety, one that by 'denaturiz[ing]' Christianity had destroyed it along with 'everything else that possesses life'.

> All living things require an atmosphere around them, a mysterious misty vapour; if

---

182 Ibid., p. 121.
183 Ibid., p. 120.
184 *SKS*. 21, NB10:169, pp. 340-341/*KJN* 8, p. 352.

> *they are deprived of this envelope, if a religion, an art, a genius is condemned to revolve as a star without atmosphere, we should no longer be surprised if they quickly wither and grow hard and unfruitful.*[185]

This was in an early work by Nietzsche, but an alternative in the shape of a 'life-view' had already been presented by Kierkegaard in his own early publication, in fact his first, *From the Papers of One Still Living*. Their shared focus is on the need to replace sheer accumulation, whether facts in science or in the case of a writer the mere serial recording of events. For this early Nietzsche, it is by blurring helpfully the distinctions that tell us that we are awake that myth saves us from the deadening sobriety of scientific thought. As a classicist he had the Greeks in mind, and it was to them that he looked for those illusions.[186] Kierkegaard, although also a classicist, and sharing the premise that to live a life as an end-in-itself takes precedence over the pursuit of knowledge, sees the solution in the form of a life-view, which is 'more than an embodiment or a sum of positions entertained in abstract indifference, more than experience which as such is always atomistic'. It is he writes, a 'transubstantiation of experience', and to someone who doesn't let their life 'fritter away too much' but tries as much as possible to turn its 'individual expressions' inwards again, there comes 'a moment when a curious illumination spreads over life'. It may not make all possible particulars intelligible, but it provides the 'key' for their 'successive understanding'.

---

185 Friedrich Nietzsche, *Unzeitgemässe Betrachtungen* (1893), ed. M. Holzinger ed., Berliner Ausgabe 2016, 93-94/*Untimely Meditations*, ed. Daniel Breazeale, trans. R. J. Hollingdale, Cambridge 1997, p. 97.

186 Friedrich Nietzsche, *Erkenntnis-theoretische Schriften*, Frankfurt 1968, p. 109.

Kierkegaard was still a student when he made these remarks and they appeared in an already typically polemical review of a book by Hans Christian Andersen, who is accused of lacking any life-view. The review was published in 1838, three years after that recreational summer vacation where in seeking his 'I' Kierkegaard had pined for an Archimedean point outside space and time. An echo of this wish appears here in talk of 'winning an unshakeable certainty' from all 'empirical experience', whether that experience is given a purely secular frame 'as in Stoicism etc.', shunning contact with a 'deeper experience', or what is taken to be 'central for both heavenly and earthly existence' is found in an 'orientation toward heaven (the religious)'. In that case, the unshakable certainty — or better said, certitude — is that of 'true Christian assurance'.[187]

The fact that piecemeal experience can be given varying depths of illumination by being transmuted into perspectives that probe ever more deeply into personal self-awareness, is something Kierkegaard would exploit in his pseudonymous works and may claim to be the 'key' to our own 'successive' understanding of these. As we know, the depths in his case produced such un-Nietzschean factors as guilt and sin-consciousness.

Readers of both writers may then ask themselves whether Nietzsche seems the more progressive of the two. The answer might be that it is he, more than Kierkegaard whose stress on the passion and supposed heroism of faith has sometimes been taken as a romantic trait, who is the true romantic. Nietzsche's own idea of what it is to live a life that is not piecemeal or atomistic breathes strongly of the optimistic and even aggressive humanism to be savoured in contemporary German

---

[187] SKS 1, pp. 32-33. The translations here my own.

philosophy at the time. Against his classicist background it even echoes the divinity-brought-to-earth perspective of the Renaissance with the promise of individual human greatness and idols not distant of the kind that Johannes Climacus mentions in connection with Religiousness A.[188]

In this context, it is the relation between the individual and the crowd that brings the comparison with Kierkegaard to a point of sharp contrast. Nietzsche could write that for him 'the masses seem to be worth a glance in only three respects: first as blurred copies of great men, presented on bad paper with worn out printing plates, then as the resistance against the great men, and finally as working implements of the great'.[189] In Kierkegaard's account the blurring is that of 'association' and 'abstract levelling'. The flight from individuality of any kind, whether superior or inferior, 'disparage[s] excellence' and prevents quite ordinary people from being 'singled out' as their own religiously oriented selves, which they can be in whatever walk of life.[190]

According to the radical theologian Karl Barth, who claimed that any system in his own thought was due to the Kierkegaardian distinction between time and eternity, what leads the individual to the idea of God as an eternal being is despair. This eternal being is the unchangeable 'ground' for which *The Sickness unto Death* nevertheless says that 'everything is possible'.[191] In any theologically interesting sense, the eternal works only within the constraints of time and space where

---

188   *SKS* 7, p. 506/*CUP*, p. 466.
189   Friedrich Nietzsche, *The Use and Abuse of History for Life*, trans. Ian. C. Johnston, Arlington VA: Richer Resources Publications, 2010, p. 52.
190   *SKS* 14, pp. 61, 80, 83/*A Literary Review*, trans. A. Hannay, London: Penguin, 2001, pp. 55, 74, 78.
191   *SKS* 11, p. 153/*The Sickness unto Death*, p. 68.

change is of the essence, the eternal then defining where our lives in inter-personal terms should be aiming. It is a target we never reach, but stretching towards it is what the eternal means to Kierkegaard's active single individual. Changes in ourselves can never make *us* eternal, yet, with time running out and change now no longer in our power, a 'repose' as close to being eternal as the confinement to time and space allows may be the best we can achieve, and possibly it is the greater the harder it has been to earn it without loss of faith. Yet, as a goal in itself, for the eternal to be outside existence it must, for those who still 'exist', remain an abstract ideal definable only by what it is not. It is timeless being and for Kierkegaard, himself and pseudonymously, its content is coded in the form of a divine love under whose light typically mundane forms of love, however harmless and inherent in humanity, are revealed as personal or social preferences, and therefore also as inherently divisive and contributing to human strife.

For Nietzsche the eternal is endless time, the 'eternal hourglass' being 'turned over again and again'. We are asked how happy we would have to become with ourselves to hope for nothing more than to do it all over 'innumerable times again' in all eternity, and in 'the same succession and sequence'. What you hear in this question are most likely the words of a 'demon', but you just might in a 'tremendous moment' say to yourself that you have never heard 'anything more divine'.[192] Nietzsche falls short of saying that this *is* divinity, but in suggesting to readers that instead of 'gnashing [their] teeth and cursing the demon who spoke thus', they might enjoy some kind of revelatory experience, he

---

192   *The Gay Science*, ed. Bernard Williams, trans. Josefine Nauckhoff, Cambridge 2001, p. 194.

appears to leave the matter open. Uncommitted readers may get the sense here of a sub-textual despair having been pushed aside, though lurking mutely in a sequel where Nietzsche asks, '[H]ow well disposed would you have to have become to yourself and to life *to long for nothing more fervently* than for this ultimate eternal confirmation and seal?'[193]

Two quotations from scripture, Pilate's 'Behold the man' (*Ecce Homo*) and Abraham's 'I am here' capture the challenges these two creatively thinking writers make to their readers.

The first was Pilate's response on an already scourged Jesus being brought again into his presence but now given a robe and crown of thorns by the soldiers and presented to the Jews as their king. Abraham's 'I am here' came twice, first in answer to God calling his name when announcing that he would test him, and again when the angel of the Lord did the same as he stood ready to sacrifice his son.

The one represents in a life of thirty-three years the cruelties of a divisive world that if they were to recur eternally would spell despair. The other offers a picture of an absolute trust that in terms of what there is every good reason to suppose will or will not happen, exceeds the bounds of sanity for anyone not mesmerised into a context-free credulity by the storyteller's art. That need be no reason to treat either as symptoms of the authors' states of mind. These are poets able to turn what hides in their hearts into telling symbols of the state of humanity. We may also bear in mind that in their time their targets were just a slice of the human cake. They were their own people, the cultured and privileged, the literati with time to read. Today matters are worse. There are those

---

[193] Ibid., pp. 194-195.

inclined to assume that Zarathustra's superior human would be unquestionably white, a symptom of a malaise that spreads further than colour and infects the entire world. The further elevation of that ideal to an abstract 'where' beyond differentiation and the constraints of time and space is an option that Kierkegaard's sympathisers might place challengingly before the followers of his fellow polemicist. In Nietzsche, the idea — or perhaps just thought experiment — of eternal recurrence recurs nowhere in the writings and there seems still to be some trace of divinity in the air, even if for Zarathustra 'God is a thought that makes crooked everything that is straight'.[194]

There are signs of open-endedness in Kierkegaard too. His startling exploitation of the Abraham image in *Fear and Trembling* as a would-be filicide ends with the venerable father of the human race cast in the now quite common role of alien, that of one who 'had to leave the land of his forefathers for a foreign land'. It is a part that the author in his life-long concern with what it means to be religious could realistically claim to have shared in his own land.

---

194   *Thus Spoke Zarathustra*, p. 66.

Bibliography

By Kierkegaard:

Søren Kierkegaards Papirer [The Papers of Søren Kierkegaard], 28 vols, ed. P. A. Heiberg, K. Kuhr and E. Torsting, Copenhagen: Gyldendal, 1909–78.
Søren Kierkegaards Skrifter [*SKS*], Bind. 1–28, Copenhagen: Søren Kierkegaard Research Centre/Gads Forlag, 1997–2011. New critical edition of Kierkegaard's book publications, journals, notebooks, newspaper articles, and correspondence (available online: sks.dk).

Kierkegaard in translation:

Kierkegaard's Writings [*KW*], 26 vols, ed. and trans. Howard V. Hong, Edna H. Hong, Henrik Rosenmeier, Reidar Thomte, and Julia Watkin, Princeton NJ: Princeton University Press, 1980-2000.
Kierkegaard's Journals and Notebooks [*KJN*], ed. Niels Jørgen Cappelørn, Alastair Hannay, David Kangas, Bruce H. Kirmmse, George Pattison, David Prossen, Joel D. Rasmussen, Vanessa Rumble and K. Brian Söderquist, vols 1–11 pts. 1 and 2), Princeton, NJ: Princeton University Press, 2007–20.

Other translations used here:

A Literary Review: Two Ages, *a novel by the author of* A Story of Everyday Life, *published by J. L. Heiberg, Copenhagen,*

Reitzel, 1843, Reviewed by S. Kierkegaard, trans. Alastair Hannay, London: Penguin Books, 2001.

The Concept of Anxiety. A Simple Psychologically Oriented Deliberation in View of the Dogmatic Problem of Hereditary Sin, trans. Alastair Hannay, New York: Liveright/W. W. Norton, 2014.

The Concept of Irony with Continual Reference to Socrates/ Notes of Schelling's Berlin Lectures, trans. Howard V. Hong and Edna H. Hong, Princeton, NJ: Princeton University Press, 1989.

Concluding Unscientific Postscript to the Philosophical Crumbs [*CUP* and *Postscript*], trans. Alastair Hannay, Cambridge: Cambridge University Press, 2009.

Eighteen Upbuilding Discourses, trans. Howard V. Hong and Edna H. Hong, Princeton, NJ: Princeton University Press, 1992.

Either/Or: A Fragment of Life, abridged and trans. Alastair Hannay, London: Penguin Books, 1992.

Fear and Trembling: Dialectical Lyric [*Fear and Trembling*], trans. Alastair Hannay, London: Penguin Books, 1985.

For Self-Examination and Judge for Yourself, trans. Howard V. Hong and Edna H. Hong, Princeton, NJ: Princeton University Press, 1990.

The Lily of the Field and the Bird of the Air: Three Godly Discourses [*The Lily of the Field and the Bird of the Air*], trans. Bruce H. Kirmmse, Princeton, NJ: Princeton University Press, 2016.

A Literary Review, trans. Alastair Hannay, London: Penguin Books, 2001.

The Moment and Late Writings [*The Moment*], trans. Howard V. Hong and Edna H. Hong, Princeton, NJ: Princeton University Press, 2009.

Papers and Journals: A Selection, trans. Alastair Hannay, London: Penguin Books, 1996.

The Point of View, trans. Howard V. Hong and Edna H. Hong, Princeton, NJ: Princeton University Press, 1998.

Practice in Christianity, trans. Howard V. Hong and Edna H. Hong, Princeton, NJ: Princeton University Press, 1991.
Repetition and Philosophical Crumbs, trans M. G. Piety, Oxford: Oxford University Press, 2009.
The Sickness unto Death, trans. Alastair Hannay, London: Penguin Books, 1989.
Upbuilding Discourses in Various Spirits, trans. Howard V. Hong and Edna H. Hong, Princeton, NJ: Princeton University Press, 1993.
Without Authority, trans. Howard V. Hong and Edna H. Hong, Princeton, NJ: Princeton University Press, 1997.

Scholarly Series Devoted to Kierkegaard:

Acta Kierkegaardiana, Kierkegaard Society in Slovakia/ Kierkegaard Circle, Trinity College, University of Toronto, 2005--.
International Kierkegaard Commentary, Macon, GA: Mercer University Press, 1984–2015.
Kierkegaardiana, Søren Kierkegaard Society, Copenhagen: C. A. Reitzel, 1955–2007.
Kierkegaard Studies Yearbook, Berlin: de Gruyter, 1996--.

Referred to and/or selected relevant works:

Arnold, N. Scott, Theodore M. Benditt and George Graham (eds), *Philosophy Then and Now*, Oxford: Blackwell, 1998.
Bobbio, Norberto, *The Philosophy of Decadentism: A Study in Existentialism*, Oxford: Blackwell, 1948.
Conway, Daniel (ed.), *Kierkegaard's Fear and Trembling: A Critical Guide*, Cambridge: Cambridge University Press, 2015.
Garff, Joakim, *Kierkegaard's Muse: The Riddle of Regine*, trans. Alastair Hannay, Princeton, NJ: Princeton University Press, 2017.

Garff, Joakim, *SAK: Søren Aabye Kierkegaard. En Biografi*, Copenhagen: Gads Forlag, 2000/*Søren Kierkegaard: A Biography*, trans. Bruce H. Kirmmse, Princeton, NJ, Princeton University Press, 2004.

Hannay, Alastair, *Kierkegaard: A Biography*, Cambridge: Cambridge University Press, 2001.

Hannay, Alastair, *Søren Kierkegaard: Critical Lives*, London: Reaktion Books, 2018.

Hannay, Alastair and Gordon D. Marino (eds), *The Cambridge Companion to Kierkegaard*, Cambridge: Cambridge University Press, 1998.

Hansen, Leif Bork, *Søren Kierkegaards Hemmelighed af Eksistensdialektik*, Copenhagen: C. A. Reitzel Forlag, 1994.

Heinesen, William, *De fortapte Spillemenn*, Copenhagen: Gyldendal, 1965.

Kirmmse, Bruce H., *Encounters with Kierkegaard: A Life as Seen by His Contemporaries* [Encounters with Kierkegaard], Princeton, NJ: Princeton University Press, 1996.

Linde, G., R. Purkarthofer, H. Schulz and P. Steinacker (eds), *Theologie zwischen Pragmatismus und Existenzdenken*, Marburg: N. G. Elwert Verlag, 2006.

Lukács, Georg, *Existentialisme ou marxisme?*, Paris: Nagel, 1948.

Marcuse, Herbert, *Reason and Revolution: Hegel and the Rise of Social Theory*, Boston: Beacon Press, 1960 (1941).

Martensen, H. L., *Christian Ethics*, trans. C. Spence (from the Danish 'with the sanction of the author'), Edinburgh, T. & T. Clark, 1873.

Martensen, H. L., *Christian Ethics*, 'Special Part: First Division: Individual Ethics', trans. William Affleck (from the author's German), Edinburgh: T. & T. Clark, 1881.

Mooney, Edward F., *On Søren Kierkegaard. Dialogue, Polemics, Lost Intimacy, and Time*, Aldershot, UK/ Burlington, VT: Ashgate Publishing Company, 2007.

Mynster, C. L. N., *Har S. Kierkegaard fremstillet de christelige Idealer – er dette Sandhed?*, foreword Jakob Paulli, Copenhagen: C. A. Reitzels Forlag, 1884.

Nietzsche, Friedrich, *Untimely Meditations*, ed. Daniel Breazeale, trans. R. J. Hollingdale, Cambridge: Cambridge University Press, 1997.

Nietzsche, Friedrich, *The Gay Science*, ed. Bernard Williams, trans. Josefine Nauckhoff and Adrian Del Caro, Cambridge: Cambridge University Press, 2001.

Nietzsche, Friedrich, *On the Genealogy of Morality*, ed. Keith Ansell-Pearson, trans. Carol Diethe, Cambridge: Cambridge University Press, 1997.

Nietzsche, Friedrich, *Thus Spoke Zarathustra*, ed. Adrian Del Caro and Robert Pippin, trans. Adrian Del Caro, Cambridge: Cambridge University Press, 2010.

Nietzsche, Friedrich, *Human, All too Human*, intro. Richard Schacht, trans. R. J. Hollingdale, Cambridge: Cambridge University Press, 1996.

Nietzsche, Friedrich, *Daybreak: Thoughts on the Prejudices of Morality*, ed. Maudemarie Clark and Brian Leiter, trans. R. J. Hollingdale, Cambridge: Cambridge University Press, 1997.

Nietzsche, Friedrich, *The Anti-Christ, Ecce Homo, Twilight of the Idols and Other Writings,* ed. Aaron Ridley and Judith Norman, trans. Judith Norman, Cambridge: Cambridge University Press, 2005.

Price, George, *The Narrow Pass: A Study of Kierkegaard's Concept of Man*, New York: McGraw Hill, 1963.

Stokes, Patrick, *The Naked Self: Kierkegaard and Personal Identity*, Oxford: Oxford University Press, 2015.

Thompson, J. (ed.), *Kierkegaard: A Collection of Critical Essays*, New York: Doubleday, 1972.

Wahl, Jean, *Études Kierkegaardiennes*, Paris: Fernand Aubier, Éditions Montaigne, 1938; Vrin 1967.

Wittgenstein, Ludwig, *Culture and Value*, ed. G. H. von Wright, trans. P. Winch, rev. ed., Oxford: Blackwell, 1998.

www.ingramcontent.com/pod-product-compliance
Lightning Source LLC
Chambersburg PA
CBHW071449250426
43671CB00043B/2576